MW01121841

PRACTICAL DREAMER:

THE GO-GETTER'S GUIDE TO CRUSH YOUR GOALS SIX WEEKS AT A TIME

PRACTICAL DREAMER

Practical Dreamer: The Go-Getter's Guide to Crush Your Goals Six Weeks at a Time

Copyright © 2021 Kalyn Brooke

All Rights Reserved. No part of this book may be reproduced or transmitted in any form without prior written consent from the author, except for the use of brief quotations in a book review.

To request permissions, contact the author at admin@kalynbrooke.com

Paperback: ISBN 978-0-9971376-2-0

Digital: ISBN 978-0-9971376-3-7

Edited by: Rachelle Cobb and Melinda Bridgman

Cover Design and Layout: Melissa Heinlein

Disclaimer:

The advice and strategies contained herein may not be suitable for your situation. You should consult with a professional where appropriate. Neither the publisher nor author shall be liable for any loss of profit or any other commercial damages, including but not limited to special, incidental, consequential, or other damages.

Due to the dynamic nature of the Internet, certain links and website information contained in this publication may have changed. The author and publisher make no representations to the current accuracy of the web information shared.

Published by KB Creative Media

KalynBrooke.com

TABLE OF CONTENTS

INTRODUCTION

It only took a year for me to say it out loud.

My husband, Joseph, and I had been working together on my online business for just that long when I threw around the idea of selling our 1,700-square-foot house in order to live and travel in an RV full-time. Joseph thought I was crazy...at first! But he slowly warmed up to the idea.

I made him watch dozens of YouTube videos featuring full-time traveling couples who were doing the exact same thing just so I could prove they weren't all hippies living out of a van. These nomads were normal, everyday people who ditched the 9-5 to live life on their terms.

Both of us share a love of traveling, but due to the work involved in growing my small business and the bills that accompany the life of a responsible adult, we had limited time and money to fuel our wanderlust. Once my business required fewer all-nighters and more everyday maintenance, our current work-from-anywhere lifestyle seemed like the perfect excuse to make the leap.

Plus, as an introverted homebody, I loved the idea of combining my love of travel with the comfort of walking into my own home. After a day at the Grand Canyon or an evening stroll through a quaint Upper Michigan downtown, we could relax on our own couch and sleep in our own bed.

It sure beat packing everything I need to survive (makeup, hair supplies, clothes, you know...the essentials!) in and out of Airbnbs the whole time.

During the next two years, we binged as much information as possible about the RV lifestyle: what we would need and what we could expect. We visited RV shows and walked through so many motorhomes that floral-patterned couches and beige walls dominated my dreams. We also decluttered our home with a vengeance and saved as much money as we could. And in the middle of it all, we second-guessed ourselves a lot too.

This was a huge life change, and we weren't sure we were ready for it!

But the one thing we didn't want to feel was regret. Regret over giving into the fear of the unknown and choosing to stay within our comfort zone. That was a risk we weren't willing to take.

And so, in the spring of 2018, we set one of our biggest life goals yet. We would start our new life on the road and say YES to full-time travel by January 2019. We just needed to sell our home and find the perfect rig before then.

A few months later, my mom called with incredible news. Her friend was selling their Fifth Wheel, and it checked off every single box on our RV wish list: the right price, the perfect length—not too small, but not too big either—a king-size bed, and my favorite feature of all, an electric fireplace to take the chill off brisk mornings.

With a rig secured, we called a realtor to officially put our home on the market. Later that fall, a family of four made an offer on our home. We picked up our new-to-us RV to start renovating the interior (goodbye, floral couch and beige walls!) and in March, we set off on the adventure of our lifetime—only two months past our initial deadline.

At this point in the story, friends, family members, and people we've met along the way all say a version of the same thing to us:

"I wish I could do something like that."

We've all at one time or another caught ourselves saying, "I wish..." haven't we?

This wistfulness often pops up while we are scrolling through social media, viewing everyone else's highlight reel through a lens of envy. Or when we're chatting with friends and you can't help but wonder how they're able to keep a clean home and work part-time and take care of three kids while still enjoying a social life. Meanwhile, you can barely get through the day.

When we encounter someone who does what we could only dream of doing, our thoughts furiously swirl with "I wish" statements. Maybe you've even caught yourself saying something like:

"I wish I was fit enough to run a 5K."
"I wish I could read that many books in a year."
"I wish I could cook healthy meals from scratch like so-and-so."

But for many of us, this desire for change comes to a screeching halt at the wishing. Something holds you back from making the next move. It could be fear of failure or indecision over where to start. The timing might not feel right. Or maybe you're not even sure what you really want and you simply feel stuck.

THE DIFFERENCE BETWEEN PROFESSIONAL AND PRACTICAL DREAMERS

If you're anything like me, you likely have no shortage of hopes and dreams buried in your heart. Joseph affectionately calls me his "grass is greener girl" because I'm always peeking over the fence, wondering how my life could be different based on the hundreds of scenarios I play out in my head.

But there is a big difference between professional dreamers and practical ones.

I bet you can think of someone who likes to talk a big game. They brag about their plans for the future, adding yet another exaggerated detail every time they repeat their story. Meanwhile, your eyes roll every time you hear it. Their timelines are often unreasonable, and they don't consider all the details needed to pull off whatever they're boasting about.

And yet their fiery personalities seem so convincing. Like whatever it is they want to do will suddenly emerge because they've passionately spoken it into existence.

But talk is cheap. Those "big talkers" almost never achieve what they *say* they're going to do because they have no practical action plan to back up their words. They are professional dreamers who would rather imagine what *could* be instead of putting in the consistent, step-by-step work to get there.

On the other hand, practical dreamers dream just as much as professional ones, but with one key difference: they bridge their desire with action.

One of my favorite podcasts is *How I Built This*. Every episode tells the story of an entrepreneur who started a well-known company— Starbucks, Whole Foods, Ben & Jerry's—and the interviews are absolutely fascinating.

In one particular interview, James Dyson[1] (yes, of Dyson vacuum fame!) shares how he turned his frustrating experience of a clogged vacuum bag into an idea for a bagless version. Five years and 5,127 prototypes later, he invented the first functional bagless vacuum cleaner that quickly became one of the top vacuum brands in the world.

Fun fact: He actually tried to license his invention to the two largest vacuum brands at the time and they wouldn't take his calls! So he started his own company. Hmmm, I wonder if they regret that decision!

But did you catch that astronomical number? James' dream didn't stop at 10, 100, or 1,000 prototypes. It took over 5,000 trial-and-error experiments for him to identify one successful version. He is the epitome of a practical dreamer. He didn't say, "Huh, I wish vacuum cleaners were bagless" and move on. He followed up that dream with a solid action plan.

I don't want you to ever be afraid to say "I wish" because you're worried that desire will never see the light. Explore those big hopes you have for your own life. Dream about all the things you really want to do!

But don't stop there.

Dreamers must become *doers*.

You must learn how to turn those dreams into reasonable, achievable goals in order to create the change you want to see in your life. And that's exactly what this book will help you do.

YOU CAN BECOME PART OF THE 8%

Before we jump into the next few chapters, consider this shocking statistic: The University of Scranton found that only 8% of people who set goals actually achieve them[2]. 8%! That means 92% of us start tackling a goal with vigor... only to have it die out later on.

Why is that? Here's my take:

1. The goal isn't that exciting or important to us. We do it (or not!) just because we think we should.
2. We set too many goals at once and bounce back and forth without making much progress.
3. We haven't found the right system to help us hit our goals out of the park.

If we know our success rate is so slim, why do we continue to make resolutions we can't keep and set goals we never finish?

Because I believe that deep within us, we hang onto a sliver of hope that things will change. That *this time* will somehow be different. And the person we want to become is closer than we think. I think so, too.

INTRODUCTION

I'm here to prove to you that you can reach any goal you set for yourself.

I pulled out my metaphorical magnifying glass and studied why some people achieve their goals while others don't. I also looked back at experiences in my own life—why some of my goals panned out and others fell flat.

Everything I discovered I am sharing with you in this book.

You'll learn the exact goal-setting process I revised for myself and for ambitious women who are juggling work, home, and other responsibilities. You'll also learn how to overcome physical and emotional hurdles like chronic illness, depression, and low energy, which I have personally struggled with but refuse to keep me from living on the sidelines.

In short, you'll go from a professional dreamer to a practical one—someone who dreams about what you could do and then turns those dreams into a tangible path to pursue.

Because achieving goals isn't just for high-achievers who seem to effortlessly manage it all and make us feel guilty for not doing enough.

Goals don't even have to be big like selling your home and moving into an RV, writing a best-selling book, or starting a work-from-home business. They can be smaller things like organizing all your digital photos, starting a recipe binder, getting in 10,000 steps a day, or practicing hospitality.

Goal-setting and goal-*getting* is for everyone.

You can become part of the 8%.

And the payoff? You'll live a life that replaces "I wish" with "I CAN." A life that empowers you to live without regrets and be proud of the person you've become.

Let's make your wildest dreams come true.

CHAPTER 1

THE GOAL-DRIVEN LIFE

If you aim at nothing, you will hit it every time. – Zig Ziglar

Every few months, a popular online article titled *"What if all I want is a mediocre life?"*[1] reenters the social media sphere like a planet in orbit, racking up thousands of shares along the way.

As you read the author's carefully penned words, you can hear the frustration and hopelessness flowing from each sentence. She has sacrificed sleep in exchange for productivity, pursued excellence to the point of exhaustion, and hates the fact that endless hustle seems to be the only way to make a massive impact on the world.

So instead of searching for middle ground, she's scurried in the opposite direction—toward a slow, simple life with an in-between body and no successful business to her name. Toward becoming a mediocre mom who rarely dusts and doesn't decorate or care about fancy things.

Because only by accepting and embracing her limitations is she able to make peace with being good enough.

I can relate to her internal struggle. Can you?

Navigating our way through a noisy and demanding world wears on us. I've found myself, on multiple occasions, treading water just to stay on top of my responsibilities and juggling looming deadlines while battling exhaustion along the way.

Sometimes, the burden of everything we have to do weighs so heavily that we find ourselves trapped in survival mode, just trying to make it through the next 24 hours playing whack-a-mole with our various tasks and responsibilities. But stay in survival mode long enough and pretty soon, you may not even care about doing your best at anything... or worse, you may give up entirely and not want to try at all.

So I understand where the author is coming from. And I find some truth in her words. *Some.*

But sit with this for a minute: The lie that we have to do it all and do it all perfectly is just that—a lie. In fact, I think it's why so many of us fail at our goals and then eventually give up setting them altogether. We're terrified of looking silly if we don't achieve what we set out to do.

No one wants to appear incompetent in front of others by admitting they've quit another 30-day challenge on day eight. Or gone over budget this month—again. Or barely made a dent in the stack of books they were going to read for the year after announcing their 40-book goal on social media.

So instead of trying again, we lower our expectations and settle in for a life of mediocrity where we can never fail.

As an overachiever who has stumbled time and time again, I get it. I understand the temptation to stay warm and cozy inside your comfort zone rather than challenge yourself to go the extra mile.

But mediocrity is not where personal growth and lasting, positive change exist. A hopeless perspective won't help you accomplish your goals or give you the fulfillment of a life well lived.

You need to first change your mindset.

LIMITING BELIEFS MAY BE HOLDING YOU BACK

Internal beliefs are extremely powerful. There's a reason for the high success rate of Cognitive Behavioral Therapy in patients struggling with anxiety and depression. This type of psychotherapy challenges negative thoughts and replaces them with positive ones in order to alter future behavior.

I underwent this therapy firsthand while fighting my own depression battle. Understanding how to identify my thoughts as a distorted perception of reality and then replace them with the truth was one of the biggest turning points in my life.

But I see these thoughts crop up in more than the mental health space. We call them limiting beliefs. Limiting beliefs cause you to doubt your *future* abilities based on perceived failures from your *past*.

Limiting beliefs reveal themselves in statements like these:

- "I never finish what I start."
- "I can't say no to sweets"
- "I'm not creative enough."
- "I never learned how to be good with money."
- "I'm terrible at relationships."

While these beliefs might seem small and insignificant, they are extremely powerful if you give them permission to stick around.

They can even become a self-fulfilling prophecy.

As an example, I used to tell myself I wasn't a runner. Every running program I started resulted in total failure. I never got the "runner's high." It was more like a "runner's groan" as I began huffing and puffing after 30 seconds of a slow jog. Meanwhile, my husband can

9

run six miles without running out of breath. I convinced myself that his body was built for running. Mine was not.

But after a particularly rough patch in my depression, I picked up the book *Running is My Therapy* and decided to try running again. Not to lose weight or to prove anything to myself. I just wanted a way to better manage my mental health.

I spent the next six months working on a four-week running program. I started running intervals one minute at a time with a one minute rest in between and worked my way up to running a 5K on Thanksgiving morning. Crossing that finish line after 40 minutes (yes, my pace is terribly slow!) of excruciating uphills and downhills wasn't going to land me in the top ten let alone top 100 of racers that day.

But I had achieved my goal of becoming a runner. Even more than that, I fell in love with running. Shocking, I know!

So what changed? What made me press on despite me saying I wasn't a runner in the very beginning?

First, I studied the craft of running. You can't get better at something unless you learn strategies from the experts. I educated myself on how to breathe properly when I run so I could run further and faster. I bought active clothes that made me feel cute and didn't inhibit my arms and legs. And I went to a running specialist for a customized shoe fitting so I had the proper foot gear.

Second and perhaps most importantly, I added the word "yet" to the end of my limiting belief.

"I'm not a runner...yet."

Do you see how that three letter word suddenly provides a mountain of hope? Let's try it out on those limiting beliefs I mentioned just a few moments earlier.

- "I never finish what I start...yet."
- "I just can't say no to sweets...yet."

- "I'm not creative...yet"
- "I can't learn how to be good with money...yet."
- "I don't do well with relationships...yet."

While you might not succeed right away (especially if you are learning something new), you always have the ability to get better and better and *better*. That little seed of confidence will grow with every step in the right direction.

Your mind is extremely powerful, so when you flip the narrative in your head, you can change your belief from limiting to unlimited. You can break out of that identity box and embrace the possibilities that open up to you once you determine that you will not be defined by a single, stifling label.

Because if you're being truly honest with yourself, those paralyzing thoughts are probably the biggest thing holding you back. Don't let them trap you into believing success isn't an option. And don't let them convince you that coasting is the best way to "get through" life.

CONTENTMENT VS. COMPLACENCY

A few months ago, I had the wonderful opportunity to meet a long-time reader face-to-face. In between sharing crocheting tips and learning about her family, she leaned over and asked me a travel-related question,

"So you've been on the road for a year...what else is there to see?"

Ohhh... so much more.

We've barely scratched the surface of our beautiful country, even though we've driven through almost every state. We've even talked about international RV travel too when we're done exploring America!

For me, travel keeps me from falling into a rut of the same thing, every day, for years. When we're ready for a change of scenery, we move.

Whether or not you feel the same way about travel, it's a healthy approach to life in general: finding ways to push yourself out of your comfort zone when things get a little too normal.

Not everyone agrees. Some naysayers like to throw around the concept of contentment as an excuse to stand still rather than move forward. You'll hear this in statements like,

- "Just be grateful for what you have!"
- "Stop striving for more!"
- "Can't you be satisfied already?"

There is some truth in this. Always looking for the next best thing is one way to miss the wonderful life you already have. It's one of the reasons why every morning, I write down five things I'm grateful for in my journal. I don't want to miss out on all the good things around me.

But there is a subtle difference between contentment and complacency.

Contentment does not require *more* to be happy. When you are content, you already have everything you need and are grateful for it, regardless of the outcome. But complacency takes contentment down a negative path. Instead of unlocking your full potential, complacency holds you back, and you wind up passively watching life drift by without any desire to change anything.

It's like tapping into the cruise control feature of your car, which Joseph loves, but I avoid entirely. For some reason, cruise control makes me feel *less* in control. Allowing the car to drive me instead of the other way around lures me into a false sense of security.

Perhaps you picked up this book because in the same way, you've allowed your life to drift on auto-pilot, slightly shifting the steering wheel when needed and stepping on the brakes only when absolutely necessary. Without a driving force of future goals, you default into a routine that lies within your comfort zone—never-changing and always focusing on dealing with what's urgent in that moment rather than carving out time for the important.

Maybe, like the author I mentioned in the beginning, you've become satisfied with a life of mediocrity.

But friend, I don't think a life of mediocrity is one you ever planned to live. Deep inside, I know you have a desire to flourish.

Benjamin Franklin once said,

> *"Without continual growth and progress, such words as improvement, achievement, and success have no meaning."*

Which means contentment and ambition do not conflict with each other when you approach the latter with the right perspective—being happy with what you have now while aiming to do better in the future.

In other words, you can still enjoy the journey without taking a backseat.

But here's an even bigger reason to challenge yourself.

LOVE THE JOURNEY JUST AS MUCH AS THE GOAL

When I first started that running program, I could have easily beaten myself up for not completing it within the designated four weeks. I was tempted to! In fact, I think most of us would admit to abandoning a goal because we're not moving at the pace we think we should.

The change you crave...you want it yesterday. And the end result doesn't look so appealing when you think of all the time and hard work it takes to get there, especially if you've been working at it for a while already.

Don't get me wrong—there is value in setting deadlines. Otherwise, we would continually procrastinate and give into the "I'll start tomorrow" mentality. Tomorrow disguises itself as a comforting friend because it promises us a fresh start the next day while giving us a pass for today. But every 'tomorrow' is just one more day of not working on your goal.

This is why my favorite goal-setting system (which I share all the details about in Chapter 5) has a built-in deadline so you can stay on track.

But the main trap I want to discuss here is thinking that the goal is the *only* measure of success. When we focus solely on the prize, we don't fully understand how much that messy, squiggly-lines-all-over-the-place middle impacts our growth. We burn ourselves out through the striving and hustling because we want to just make it to the finish line already.

For professional athletes, one would assume that winning games and making it to the final championship should be the ultimate goal. Not true according to the late tennis player, Arthur Ashe, who became a famous role model for the Black community.

He's credited with saying, "Success is a journey, not a destination. The doing is often more important than the outcome."

Even when he was inducted into the Virginia Sports Hall of Fame in 1979, the Hall said (in a similar, but more long-winded way[2]),

"Arthur Ashe was certainly a hero to people of all ages and races, and his legacy continues to touch the lives of many today. For Arthur Ashe, tennis was a means to an end. Although he had a lucrative tennis career, it was always more than personal glory and individual accolades. He used his status as an elite tennis player to speak out against the moral inequalities that existed both in and out of the tennis world. Ashe sincerely wanted to bring about change in the world. What made him stand out was that he became a world champion along the way."

Winning...is not everything. Reaching a goal...is not everything.

It's true, goals provide you with a sense of purpose and direction for your life so you don't coast along waiting for things to happen to you. But this end point also exists for you to look back and see how you've developed personally in a positive way. Which if you follow this logic, makes the PROCESS of achieving your goal just as important (if not moreso!) than the goal itself.

Think about it.

- The journey of losing weight also helps you build healthy habits that can continue for a lifetime.
- When you write a book, you often discover more about yourself through the process, not because you're holding a published manuscript in your hands.
- As you read more, you gain ideas and insight based on what you learned, which has nothing to do with the quantity of books on your list.

Do you see where I'm going here? If you love the journey just as much as the goal, you're already successful because of the skills you've acquired, connections you've made, and the person you've become, whether you ever achieve that final goal or not.

So as you approach goal-setting based on the dreams and desires you envision for your life, learn to welcome and appreciate those experiences along the way. You don't need to charge toward the finish line to develop good, life-changing goals and habits.

You just need to take one small step today and the next day and the next.

Each step will teach you much more about the value of the process than instant results ever will. And when you're tempted to give up because you're not going fast enough, remember that you're still moving in the right direction.

CHAPTER 2

SETTING GOALS THAT MATTER

Comparison is the thief of joy – Theodore Roosevelt

One day, I had a crazy *non-morning* person idea. My first book deadline hovered over me like a dark cloud threatening a nasty storm and I knew I couldn't possibly finish the draft in time unless I added three more hours to my day.

There was no other choice—I had to wake up earlier.

I noticed that everyone seemed to respect morning people more than their night owl counterparts...including well-known brands like Delta airlines.

In 2017, Delta launched a commercial titled "4am,[1]" which featured Viola Davis as the voiceover while the iconic Disney song "Heigh Ho" played in the background. On social media, they shared this video alongside the caption: "The ones who truly change the world are the ones who can't wait to get out in it."

In summary, if you wake up early, you are a power player who will accomplish important things in the world. If you wake up at 7am or later, you're viewed as lazy, unmotivated, and unproductive.

Not wanting to adopt any of those negative traits, I joined the 5am club.

The 5am club is an exclusive group of people who, inspired by Robin Sharma's book of the same name, get up at 5am every day. These early risers have one goal—to wake up early and make the most out of each day. That "most" depends on the person. Maybe they want to focus on a particular pursuit (personal growth, health, etc.), or they simply desire to start their day peacefully instead of feeling rushed.

With my book deadline in mind, I excitedly set my alarm to chirp a happy tune at 5am sharp. I settled into my comfy pillow, pulled up the blanket around my chin, and blissfully fell asleep.

That bliss was short-lived as 5am quickly arrived and my once happy-sounding, now annoying alarm jolted me out of a deep coma-like sleep. Despite every bone in my body shouting at me to stay under the covers, I reminded myself why I was doing this.

I shuffled into my home office brushing cobwebs from my eyes while muttering my goal over and over to remind myself why I was doing this. Then I flipped on the light and got to work.

For three (very long) weeks, I maintained this habit. And during the first few days, the results were pretty surprising.

- I loved how productive I felt.
- I loved that my hardest task was out of the way before breakfast.
- I loved that I was part of this exclusive "morning club" and felt like a total rockstar. Just like Delta predicted, I was changing the world!

But those feelings didn't last. A couple weeks into my new morning routine, I crashed...and burned.

My body couldn't sustain the 5am wake up time for very long, even though every so-called personal development expert all but guaranteed I could become a "morning person" if I did x, y, and z. I now have a strong suspicion that those early risers are excessively chipper morning people for whom waking up early comes natural. However, back then, I began to wonder, "Is something wrong with me? Am I just not cut out to be an 'early bird'?"

Rewatching that Delta commercial, maybe they didn't mean to discriminate against non-morning people, but knowing what I know now, it's how I took their less-than-motivational message. Turns out, I had bought into the lie of absolutes: setting goals based on what everyone else thought I should do rather than what I *wanted* to do.

SAY GOODBYE TO "SHOULD"

I'm about to make a pretty bold statement. Are you ready?

Here it is: "Should" is one of the most dangerous words in the English dictionary. In fact, I'd lump it right along with the words "ought to," "need to," "have to," "supposed to," and "must." Whether or not you agree with me, allow me to share where I'm coming from.

I believe words like these add unnecessary pressure to do something you may or may not want to do, accompanied by a guilt-ridden road trip if you don't follow through. These words don't inspire you to action; they merely remind you of every obligation you've placed on yourself based on what *you* think you should do or obligations based on what other people think you should do.

In short, they make you feel utterly and completely inadequate.

But how many of us set goals based on the "shoulds" in our life? This mindset was exactly why I chose to wake up at 5am each morning. Not because I wanted to... I thought I *had* to. It was the only way I thought I could write a book.

I know differently now. But maybe like me, you've struggled with this temptation in the past.. You've given the word "should" and it's obligatory-sounding friends an unhealthy amount of attention.

Maybe you told yourself you *had* to lose weight so you could avoid buying jeans in the next size up. Or you *should* pick up a book instead of your phone when you're bored. Or you were *supposed* to start that family yearbook because your mother-in-law insists your phone isn't the place to keep all those memories.

Do you feel enthusiastic about following through on any of those goals simply because you "should" do all those things? Um, I don't!

As well-meaning as you might be in wanting to grow and change in a positive way, using absolutes like "have to," "supposed to," and "must" readies your inner rebel for battle. Call in the resistance! Because nobody (not even yourself) gets to tell you what to do.

For some of us, it goes even further. Our subconscious fights back with self-sabotaging behavior, just to prove that we're the boss.

Take food as an example.

Imagine telling yourself after an excessive brownie binge that you should never eat dessert again. Okaaay, that's really heartbreaking... no more brownies?!

But here's the deal: restricting any kind of food makes that particular food more desirable, which can trigger overeating. This "one-time" binge starts a vicious cycle of guilt-led undereating the next day and intensifies your hunger for the forbidden food.

Suddenly, tasting one small morsel of brownie compels you to devour the whole pan.

The authors of the book *Intuitive Eating* have seen this happen to their clients time and time again. And they came up with a brilliant (albeit suspicious in my mind!) solution: Give yourself unconditional permission to eat the forbidden food.

This permission eliminates the urgency to overeat because you're not telling yourself no forever. You can have another brownie tomorrow and the next day and the next.

Which sounds great! But if you allowed yourself to eat a brownie every day for the rest of your life, you would inevitably get sick of brownies. I know that sounds impossible, but track with me here. The novelty of the food wears off when you don't give yourself an ultimatum to avoid it entirely.

So how does this relate to your goals? Besides eating brownies as a reward when you complete them?

Instead of telling yourself what you should and should not do (which will send you running in the opposite direction), I want you to replace those words with more empowering ones like "choose," "get to," and "can."

Let's try it:

· "I have to workout today" vs "I *get* to workout today"
· "I'm supposed to lose 20 pounds" vs "I *will* lose 20 pounds"
· "I should start an Emergency Fund" vs "I *choose* to start an Emergency Fund"

Did you catch that subtle difference? Already, the pressure to live up to an unattainable standard is gone. What a relief!

But there's one more step that is even more important than saying goodbye to the "shoulds" and "must do's" in your life. I want you to evaluate what *is* important to you (and more specifically why) so you're not tempted to fall into that trap of uninspiring obligations again.

In other words, you want to choose goals that align with your priorities and core values. It's the only way you'll be committed enough to follow through.

Because maybe the things you think you *should* do don't align with what you actually want.

THE IMPORTANCE OF YOUR CORE VALUES

When you think of the term "core values", what comes to mind? For me, I can't help but envision a boring investment company who passes out marketing brochures filled with pithy sayings like, "Save for the future!" and "We take a holistic approach to your finances!"

Core values often aren't something (as a customer) that you really think or care about.

I mean, when was the last time you mulled over Starbucks' mission and value statements while waiting in the drive-through for a Salted Caramel Mocha with coconut milk and three shots of espresso? Probably never. You just want the smooth liquid gold sliding down your throat STAT.

Yet almost every well-known company has them. Have you ever wondered why?

For one, core values keep fellow team members on the same page. One of Starbucks' many values is[2]: "Creating a culture of warmth and belonging, where everyone is welcome." So if you're a barista who has a nasty habit of talking back to customers, Starbucks has every right to fire you. You're not acting according to the environment they want to portray.

Perhaps more importantly, values help guide a company's decisions. Since I don't have an inside look into the top-level decisions Starbucks makes (although that would be interesting), I'll use my own business as an example.

Yep, even though it's just myself and a small team working behind the scenes, I still have a set of business values.

They're quite simple, actually.

· Always be kind
· Push through adversity
· Never stop learning

So when I receive a comment about how I sit around on the computer and do nothing every day (true story!), I need to respond with kindness. When my site crashes overnight and I wake up to a mess the next morning (another true story!) I need to limit the panic, focus on the problem, and find a solution. And since education is vitally important to my continued growth, I'm almost always working through an online business course.

But I would argue that core values are not just for companies, big or small. Everyone has them, even you. Maybe you haven't specifically defined your values yet (they're not always tangible, after all), but they're still there, popping up in the things, people, and experiences you care about most.

You might have grown up with a set of values from your parents or a favorite teacher or a coach. Over time as you encounter people you admire and read books that expand your horizons, your values might grow stronger, shift a little, or be replaced entirely.

But no matter what your values are, these guiding principles help define what you stand for, who you want to be, and how you want to live. And just like big companies and well-known brands, they provide guidelines for almost every decision you make.

As an example, let's say you receive an unexpected bonus at work. Congrats! But how will you spend your bonus? Will you put the money toward a future vacation? Beef up your emergency fund? Rush into HomeGoods to gather all the lovely things you saw last week but didn't buy?

This isn't a choice between right and wrong. It's a choice between what you value more—a travel opportunity or financial security or a pretty home? Your values always determine where you spend your money.

I put the emphasis on *you*, because if you took this question to your group of friends, you would get a variety of answers. Some might agree with your decision while others would use the money in a different way. That's because values vary person to person. Your core values are not the same as your mom's/sister's/husband's/best friend's. They're 100% yours.

It's important to make this distinction before you rush toward a goal that doesn't hold personal significance for you. Picking a goal at random or because a pretty social media account guilted you into doing so, will only lead to maddening frustration on your end.

But when you define your values, you're more likely to set goals *based* on those values. And you'll be more committed (and excited!) to follow through because you're not setting this goal for anyone else but yourself.

TAKING STOCK: A LIFE INVENTORY ASSESSMENT

So how do you define your core values? Do you pluck important-sounding words out of thin air and set goals based on what sounds good?

Some people do. They print out a master list and claim the words that speak most to them. Words like authenticity, compassion, loyalty, reputation, trustworthiness, self-respect, and creativity.

But I prefer a different approach.

For one, you can't always sum up your values in one word (or two!). It's also really difficult to know what *authenticity* and *loyalty* look like in real life. Words have power, sure, but these are just words without context.

So instead of choosing a word, I recommend doing a Life Inventory Assessment. By dividing your life into seven major areas and measuring your level of satisfaction in each, you will get a detailed picture of what's important to you and where you want to improve.

Let's define them first.

1. **Relationships** - Think about all the relationships in your life, not just your children or a significant other. You have family, friends, and coworkers too! As social creatures, we need to maintain happy and healthy relational connections to thrive.

2. **Health** - When we hear the word "health," most of us immediately examine our food intake and exercise, but I also want you to pay attention to how you feel emotionally and spiritually. All aspects of your health directly impact whether you'll have a positive or negative experience throughout the day.

3. **Career** - Your job could be inside or outside the home, but either way, the work you do matters. And we all want to be fulfilled in our work! Consider if you want (or need) to make any changes in this area, from a completely new career to trying something new in the job you currently have.

4. **Finances** - When it comes to money, think through all aspects of your financial situation—your current budget, expenses, debt, and savings goals, then zero in on the most pressing issue for you right now. Or maybe you're further along in your financial journey and want to find ways you can give back or be more financially independent.

5. **Physical Environment** - Don't underestimate the power of your current surroundings and their effect on your mood and productivity. Take a good look around your home to see how you could better organize an area, declutter to open up your space, or change anything from paint colors to throw pillows to create a more inspiring environment.

6. **Personal Development** - Self-improvement is an ongoing process because to grow, you need to learn. And there's always something new to learn! Here's where you'll pinpoint your strengths and weaknesses in order to better understand who

you are and who you want to be.

7. **Fun and Recreation** - You can probably think of various hobbies or other leisure activities that you enjoy, like traveling, reading, drawing etc. (Or maybe I should say would enjoy more if you had more time to pursue them!) This life area rounds out the rest so you don't forget to prioritize fun.

Now the real work begins.

We need to honestly evaluate how you're doing in each life area so we can compare your current reality to where you'd like to be in the future. We're basically taking a snapshot of your life right now to create a detailed picture of where you are and where you want to go. This will help you identify goals that point you in the right direction.

For instance, in the Relationship category, maybe you immediately thought of a friend you lost touch with over the years with whom you'd love to reconnect. A Relationship goal could be to set a reminder on your phone to text her once a week just to see how she's doing.

Or you realized that you really want to work from home, so in the Career category, you could look for virtual job opportunities or possibly even start your own business.

These observations are exactly what I want you to capture during this assessment. But don't worry, I'm not leaving you stranded without any guidance! Grab a blank notebook or The Six-Week Sprint Goal Planner, which you may have purchased as a companion guide to this book, and answer these three important questions as you assess every life area on the list:

1. *What is working right now?* Negativity can often make you feel like a failure and that you have so much work ahead of you, which is why I want you to first identify what you are doing well in every area. You are excelling in far more ways than you think!

2. *What frustrates you the most?* Think of a problem area that if you

could solve it, it would have a ripple effect on other parts of your life.

3. *What do you wish you had more time for?* In your ideal world, write down activities or projects that you would tackle if you had more hours in the day. Consider not just today, but 3-5 years from now. What do you want to have accomplished?

Whew! Who knew three questions packed such a punch?

It's okay if you need a few days to complete this exercise. I don't want you to rush and miss the personal insight that comes from deep soul work. And to go deep, you need time. Answering these questions *fully* and *honestly* is vital to choosing goals that will seamlessly integrate into your life and motivate you to action.

When you're finished and begin reading over your answers, you might feel a little overwhelmed as you think about the big changes you want to see. Some of these changes might even feel like a pipe dream. You can't envision them coming to life because you're not even sure where to start. Or maybe you're worried you dreamed too big!

Let what I'm about to say assure you. You don't need to tackle every life change just because you wrote it down and most certainly not all at once. In fact, I don't even want you to try that. Because you will achieve more goals in the same time period if you focus on just one, rather than two or three at a time.

In the next chapter, I'll explain how to further narrow down your goals to find one that is perfectly aligned with your core values. I promise this process will be insightful and fun!

But for right now, remember that *your* values drive *your* goals. If your assessment uncovers a goal that sounds like it might be for you, but deep down external or internal pressure is driving your reasoning, let it go. Move on. Live a life you're proud of rather than hopelessly trying to gain the approval of others.

Set the goals that mean the most to YOU and you'll increase the chance of your success before you even start.

CHAPTER 3

WHAT GOAL SHOULD YOU FOCUS ON FIRST?

Success is built sequentially. It's one thing at a time. – Gary Keller

Goals add so much meaning and purpose to life, especially when they are connected to your purpose *in life*. But too much of a good thing can quickly turn into a damaging thing. Like when you try to achieve multiple goals at the same time.

On the surface, setting more than one goal makes sense. If you want to move forward in multiple life areas, you must see progress in multiple life areas... or so the goal-setting gurus say. No one wants to neglect their relationships or health for the sake of work and vice versa.

So in search of the world's unrealistic vision of a balanced life, we set out to change everything about ourselves that we assume needs work.

Here's the problem, though.

Balance prevents you from "going all in" on anything. Balance chains you to the middle so you can avoid the extremes of the right and left, never committing a significant amount of time to any one area of your life. If you approach your list of possible goals with balance, each one will tug at you, claiming just as much importance as the next. And equal approaches almost never result in equal outcomes.

It took a loooooong time for me to learn this. Every goal-setting experience would turn disastrous whenever my idealistic side overruled my realistic side. My most recent mishap was just over a year ago when I set four rather large goals at one time.

I had just finished reading a fascinating book about goal setting and immediately turned to a crisp blank page in my bullet journal to sketch out which goals I wanted to tackle first.

Two goals would help me grow my online business—a new product launch and evergreen email campaign—while the others were of a more personal nature—building my $1,000 emergency fund to $2,000 and assembling a Dessert Recipe Binder. To me, this sounded like the ideal combination of work and personal goals.

I started out strong, jumping back and forth between my goals as I accomplished one task after another. But a few weeks later, I gave up on my goals entirely. My digital product was partially complete, my emergency fund had only increased by an extra $200, and I still hadn't touched the email campaign or recipe binder.

My exhaustion turned into frustration when I realized that after weeks of work, I still couldn't check off one goal. Multitasking (or should I say multi-goaling?) didn't work. Rather than save time, I *wasted* it. And I had very little to show for the time I did spend.

Just because you can set multiple goals, doesn't mean you should.

But in today's fast-paced world, no one wants to hear that multitasking doesn't work.

You might disagree with me. Maybe you've listened to a podcast while cooking dinner or you often knock out a few things on your to-do list while chatting on the phone. But in reality, when you're multitasking, your brain flits back-and-forth between tasks without giving full attention to either one.

Your cooking goes on autopilot as you tune into an interesting phrase from your podcast. And while you're focused on measuring ingredients, the podcast slowly fades into the background. But your brain switches so quickly, you may not even notice the back-and-forth.

In *The One Thing*, authors Gary Keller and Jay Papasan compare multitasking to juggling.

"Juggling is an illusion. To the casual observer, a juggler is juggling three balls at once. In reality, the balls are being independently caught and thrown in rapid succession. Catch, toss, catch, toss, catch, toss. One ball at a time. It's what researchers refer to as 'task switching.'"

So while you may *think* you can concentrate on two things at once, your brain can only focus on one thing at a time. And every time you switch activities (whether it's mere seconds or minutes in between), you're sending your already exhausted brain through a series of mental gymnastics as it adjusts to its new role.

Our goals are not immune to this phenomenon.

Lean in, because here comes the pep talk. If you *try* to juggle ten goals at once (which you now know is impossible), you'll set yourself up for failure.

Limiting yourself to one goal feels so counterintuitive if you are a go-getter who wants to do all the things. But when you leverage your focus on one goal, you're fully committed to achieving that goal without getting distracted trying to make progress on another goal at the same time.

Think about it.

You wouldn't need to eat healthy and exercise more and read 40 books and start a journaling habit and declutter your entire house in January. You could breathe a sigh of relief as you choose the *one goal* that meant the most to you and go all in on that one goal until you cross the finish line.

I guarantee you'll knock out your goal quicker than you ever thought possible. And that success will inspire you to set another goal and another and another. By the end of the year, you could cross the finish line on six total goals because you flipped the myth of multitasking on its head by doing the complete opposite.

You focused.

But how will you ever narrow all your dreams down to one?

REMEMBER YOUR SEASON OF LIFE

I tend to look at life in seasons. Not the ones that probably popped into your mind—Spring, Summer, Fall, and Winter—although anyone who has school-age children knows how busy Fall is versus the Summer months!

Instead, I define life seasons by what is happening in your life right now. Some seasons allow for more activities; others require you to scale back to just the essentials.

For the longest time, I said no to a lot of things (sometimes even cleaning my house—gross, I know) in lieu of writing and doing the million other things that come from building a successful online business. When I could hire out tasks and set up systems so my business didn't require all my attention, I brought back some of those daily habits I had left behind.

But it took time. *Years*, even. If I had tried to do everything at once (build my business, keep a sparkling clean home, volunteer at church, etc,) I wouldn't have done anything well. I had to scale back on other things to focus on my *one* thing.

If you've ever watched *Fixer-Upper*, then you're familiar with farmhouse-style pioneer Joanna Gaines. Long before this show launched Chip and Joanna into an American household name, she ran a little shop called Magnolia Market.

In her shop, Joanna sold vintage finds that define the decor she's most known for today. But when she was pregnant with her second child, she felt God leading her to shut everything down and focus on raising her growing family.

That must have been one of the hardest decisions of her life. And yet, she trusted God that her dreams were not gone...they were just on hold. And one day, He would open up doors that were bigger than she could even imagine.

During those early child-rearing years, Chip and Joanna worked together as a team on their construction business, Magnolia Homes. A few years later, HGTV contacted them about doing the show *Fixer-Upper*. More than 3 million viewers tuned in to watch the couple renovate homes, and soon after, Joanna felt the nudge to reopen her little shop.

Which has since expanded to the Magnolia Silos, a popular tourist destination in Waco, Texas.

Joanna probably felt as if her dreams had been shattered the day she closed her market's doors, but they were renewed in an extraordinary way when her kids were a little older and she entered a new life season.

Maybe you have young children and in this season of life they are your priority right now. Or perhaps you are caring for an elderly parent. You could be busy moving into a new home, volunteering at a food pantry once a week, or holding down a part-time job in the evenings.

Remember this: your life season is not a life sentence. There is a cycle to everything. Leaves bloom and then fall a few months later. Nature shifts every few months and so will you, with each season contributing to your growth in some way even if it wasn't what you originally envisioned.

So as you glance down your exhaustive list of all the things you wish were different, don't forget—saying no to something now doesn't mean no forever. Just because you're pushing all the rest of your goals aside doesn't mean you don't care about them. Or that you'll never work on them again.

You're actually doing your other goals a favor by leaving them on the sidelines. When you tell yourself that now is not the time to focus on a goal because you can't give your goal the 100% attention it deserves, you respect your current commitments as well as the time and effort it requires.

And you'll start to narrow your long list of possible goals down to a manageable handful.

FIND THE LOGICAL OVERLAP

After setting aside goals that are not right for this season, perhaps only 2-3 remain on your list. If these goals don't sound too hard or time-intensive, you might be tempted (again!) to tackle both at once.

I have to remind myself daily that my focus directly impacts my results. Even when I'm working through a massive to-do list that has nothing to do with my current goals, I still feel the tug to multitask. But when I focus on one task versus bits and pieces of them all, I notice a phenomenal difference in my "done" list.

Ahem... there's a lot more on it.

So when deciding between 2-3 tempting goals, I find it helpful to answer this three-part question: **what will have the greatest positive impact in your life at this moment in the shortest amount of time and is the one you are most excited about?**

The intersection of these elements is where you'll find your answer.

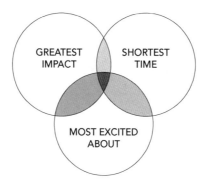

For example, let's say after glancing over my own life inventory list, I want to:
1. Renovate the bathroom
2. Create a capsule wardrobe
3. Redesign my website
4. Declutter my closet
5. Build an emergency stockpile of food

I could argue that the goal with the greatest impact would be to renovate the bathroom. It would make getting ready in the morning easier. Or I could create a capsule wardrobe to minimize clutter and help me feel more confident about putting outfits together. Or I could redesign my website, which would be better organized for readers and possibly bring in more traffic.

Decluttering my closet would take the shortest amount of time—a weekend at most.

But I'm also most excited about creating a capsule wardrobe. Stockpiling food? Necessary, but *boring*.

In the end, I could easily combine two goals into one—I could declutter my closet first (which doesn't take a lot of time), then build a capsule wardrobe to replace the pieces I donated (which is what I'm most excited about and will have the greatest immediate impact).

Albeit in two parts, this is my goal.

Are you starting to see how this works?

Take a moment to comb through your own life inventory list, remembering what's possible in your current life season and then answering the three-part question I mentioned earlier. The answer may reveal itself right away or you'll need a few days to process this exercise in your notebook or The Six-Week Sprint Goal Planner.

You might even second guess yourself too. Is there such a thing as one perfect goal?

As a perfectionist and Enneagram 1, I'd love to think so. Following a set of rules all but guarantees I'm on the right path, right? I'm most comfortable when I *know* I'm doing the right thing.

But I can't support one goal being significantly better than the other ... because it's not true.

You can make all the arguments based on your current life season. You could send your goal through a series of flow charts and diagrams, hoping to see the perfect goal emerge at the end. It's good to do those things when you're overwhelmed over the dozens of goal-setting possibilities.

What really matters, though, is choosing a goal that matters to you. Which one do *you* think is the most important?

Because when you choose one goal, whatever that goal is, you are telling yourself (and others!) that this goal is a priority. That's what makes it the right goal. Nothing else. Use the tools I've given you. But then you have to make a final decision. You have to commit.

Going after any goal is hard work. Don't make it more difficult by choosing more than one.

SUCCESS BUILDS OVER TIME

Tackling one goal at a time will take time. But whenever you're tempted to compare your progress to someone else's, remember: there is no such thing as overnight success.

That business owner built a successful business *over time*. That inspirational speaker developed her persuasive skills *over time*. That hobbyist knitter who now owns a thriving Etsy shop selling patterns learned how to knit and market her products over time.

So even though it feels like you're growing slow, you're building your own version of "over time."

Many people are surprised that I made very little money the first two years of my online business. I still put in 20-30 hour weeks (I was working at the time and blogged in the evenings and on weekends). But I walked away with pennies for my effort.

And yet, I kept plugging away, night after night, weekend after weekend. Was I discouraged? Of course! Many nights, I cried myself to sleep over the crickets surrounding my newly published blog post or my Amazon affiliate account with $3.49 in it—same as last month and the month before that.

But I saw multiple online business owners who brought in full-time incomes after years of hard work. If they could do it, that meant I could do it too. And after four years, I finally earned that full-time income. Now eight years later, we are using that income to fuel our full-time travel dreams.

When people ask me how I built such a sustainable business or they want to start a similar business and are looking for advice, I always tell them a version of the same thing. I built it over time. That's not what most people want to hear. They want marketing secrets that will help them make $1,000 the next day.

And when they don't see instant progress, they give up.

I don't want that to be you.

So before you move onto the next chapter, before we send your goal through a refining process to gain crystal clear clarity over your one goal, take a moment to embrace this new mindset.

Remember that every action step forward adds up over time. At a certain point, other people will look at you and wonder how you managed to read so many books in a year or completely overhaul your eating habits or create twelve family yearbooks.

The answer? You did it...over time.

But in the *meantime*, you must ensure your goal is an A.C.T.ual goal.

CHAPTER 4

A.C.T.UAL GOALS

You can't build a reputation on what you're going to do. – Henry Ford

Years ago when our RV dream was still just that (a dream), we bought a 4-bedroom house in Florida. As potential homebuyers, I'll never forget the moment when we first opened the front door and followed our real estate agent inside.

Immediately, everything about this home felt right. I even shouted, "This is our house!" I was already envisioning how I would arrange the furniture, making a mental list of new artwork I needed to buy and trying to decide which color blue to paint on the living room walls—Tidewater or Sea Salt?

In our previous home (which was a duplex that we planned to rent out), I made decorating decisions based on what the majority of renters would enjoy. I chose neutral paint colors and flooring because that home was an investment.

A bad one, as I discovered later on, but that story is for another book!

With so many bedrooms in *this* house, I could finally design the home office of my dreams. And since the office housed a fairly large closet, I could turn that additional space into the perfect craft storage oasis. Currently, most of my supplies were a disorganized mess, which promptly discouraged any desire to DIY. A craft closet would change everything.

I gathered ideas from magazines and clipped photos online, all the while imagining drawers full of tidy washi tape rows and organized files of patterned paper and stickers.

But for two full years, I did nothing to further my goal of "create an organized craft closet." This goal floated around as a vague idea in my head because I didn't take the time to define what an organized craft closet actually looked like. Nor did I break down the steps to get there or give myself a deadline to complete it.

This isn't unusual.

More often than not, what seems like a worthy-sounding goal *at first* ever so slightly misses the mark. Take these "goals" for example: I want to eat healthier, workout more, and maintain a consistently clean home. But ...

What does eating healthier look like? How many times a week do you want to work out and what kind of workouts do you plan to complete? What does a "clean home" mean to you? Do you need to clean every day or once a week?

Most importantly, how will you know when you've reached your goal?

If these questions feel unnecessary (or overly inquisitive), you're not alone. Many people set goals that are too lofty and too vague without a clearly defined target. It's not natural to approach every goal with extreme specificity.

That's because in our eagerness to set new goals, we're lured into thinking that details don't matter. If you want to achieve something significant, you write it down in the goals section of your new planner. Or you create a vision board. Or you announce your hopes and intentions on social media alongside a carefully arranged flat lay photograph that would rival anyone's in the planner community.

I'm not knocking any of these things. Inspiration and accountability do make a difference. But I'm afraid we spend so much time focusing on the end result, that we forget to prioritize how we're going to get there.

And it starts with turning your *vague idea* of a goal into an A.C.T.ual goal.

You've already chosen a goal worth pursuing. Now your goal needs clarity. Specifically, your goal needs three crucial elements to turn it into an achievable target. When you know exactly where you're aiming, you'll hit the bullseye every time.

I call this entire process the A.C.T. Method.

1. Your goal must be **A**ttainable. I'm all for setting big goals—reach for the stars, I say! But what we often miss are the small, stepping stone goals that make up a bigger goal. I'll show you how to keep that big goal in mind while establishing milestones along the way.
2. Your goal must contain a **C**lear, measurable target. Vague goals have no place here. We will define your goal in detail so you can maximize your chance of success.
3. Your goal must also include a **T**ime-trigger—a frequency of how often you will work on your goal or a final deadline.

Assigning each of these elements to your goal will automatically make it easier to achieve because now, you've defined a clear-cut objective. Let's explore each section of the A.C.T. Method in detail so you can see how this works in real life.

YOUR GOAL MUST BE ATTAINABLE

I'm the type of person who loves setting aspirational goals. I shudder when I hear the word "attainable" because to me, it sounds like a cap on the ceiling of my life. You mean to tell me I can't dream big? That I have *limits*? No way.

But that's not the case at all.

You can set big goals that are attainable. The two are not mutually exclusive. But you need to find the sweet spot between a goal that is achievable and one that pushes you outside your comfort zone.

Here's why.

If your goal is too small, you'll settle for doing less than you're capable of and actually hold yourself back. Human nature wants us to avoid failure as much as possible, and big goals might hurl you down that discouraging path at top speed. So in response, you scale down your goal until there's no question you can accomplish it.

But if you have no doubt you can reach a goal, what will compel you to wake up in the morning and pursue that goal with everything you have? With a larger goal, you subconsciously change your attitude from "I've totally got this" to "Whoa, I better get to work!" You have to prioritize your goal on the calendar if you want to get it done.

In other words, your efforts directly correlate to the size of your goal.

The reality show, *Shark Tank*, perfectly illustrates this phenomenon. Five multi-millionaire listen to business pitches from hopeful entrepreneurs and decide whether or not to invest their own money.

Provided everything goes well, the entrepreneur not only receives exposure for their product or service, they also get a chance to work with a high-profile businessman or woman who has enviable connections with some of the world's biggest brands.

But there's one mistake almost every entrepreneur makes—they offer too little equity to the sharks because they fear giving away too much of their company in exchange for cash. And do you know what the sharks say...every time?

"5% is not going to motivate me to work on your behalf."

The sharks invest their money in hundreds of other companies. If they own 40% of a business vs 5%, where do you think they will invest more of their time and effort? The higher equity beats out the lower every time.

So take a good look at the goal you've chosen. If it feels a tiny bit scary, you've struck gold. Otherwise, I'd encourage you to bump it up a notch until you feel slightly uncomfortable. Instead of working out 3x a week, shoot for 4x. Instead of saving for a $1,000 emergency fund, increase it to $2,000. Goals should compel you to take massive action.

However, if you've already set a really big goal, such as running a marathon, writing a book, or learning a new language, you'll need to break that goal down into milestones. If a goal is too big, you'll experience overwhelm at all the steps required to get there. Milestones keep you working toward a bigger goal with mini accomplishments and celebrations along the way.

Going back to my craft closet, I was attempting a rather large goal—one I couldn't accomplish all at once. So I narrowed my focus down to one significant milestone—organizing my gift supplies—and went to work sketching how that part of my closet would come to life. This milestone brought me one step closer to my big goal and gave it a more specific objective.

Which leads me to my next point.

YOUR GOAL MUST BE CLEAR AND MEASURABLE

With your attainable, yet slightly uncomfortable goal in mind, now you need to narrow your focus into a clear, well-defined goal that is easily measurable. All too often, we find ourselves floundering in the middle of our goal wondering how we'll ever reach the other side. Starting a goal is almost never the problem. Completing a goal is the difficult part!

And when it comes to meeting your goal, you should know without a doubt that you have achieved it or not, and if not, how much further you have to go. A goal that is clear and measurable means you can easily track your progress based on the specific outcome of your goal.

People are often confused about the difference between a goal, a task, and a habit, so it's worth defining that more specifically here before we move on. These definitions will also help you know how to confidently apply the goal setting system in the next chapter.

Tasks are short and doable. You should be able to check off a task in a matter of minutes or, at most, a couple of hours. Tasks are not a grand achievement as much as they are part of a workflow like daily chores or prepping your kids to go back to school.

Meanwhile, a large series of tasks are what make up a larger goal, which can either be an achievement goal or habit-based.

You're probably more familiar with achievement goals because they offer a clearly defined end point, like running a marathon or writing a book. You know for sure whether or not you have achieved your goal. You either run the marathon, or not. And you finish writing your book, or not.

A habit-based goal represents ongoing activity, like running 3x per week or writing 500 words a day. You practice these habits so often and so regularly, they eventually become a way of life.

But habits and goals can also go hand-in-hand.

You can't necessarily run a marathon if you haven't implemented the habit goal of running a certain amount each week. Or if you did, it would be very difficult! The same principle applies to writing and publishing a book. Writing on a consistent basis (for example, 500 words per day) will eventually lead to you writing a 50,000 word manuscript.

Knowing the difference between achievement goals and habit goals will help you know which one to choose based on the end result you want—a final endpoint or consistent practice—and whether or not you need a combination of both to cross that finish line.

When I set a goal of an organized craft closet and later modified that goal to cover just my gift-wrapping supplies, I created an achievement goal. My clear outcome was an organized gift supply section with boxes for bows, a modified crate to hold wrapping paper, and one gift bag to hold all my other gift bags.

But to make consistent, measurable progress, I needed to work on some aspect of this project every week. So I added a task to my weekly to-do list (like decluttering my current supplies or sketching my vision on graph paper) and then later on, assigned that task to a specific day.

Let's look at another example—building an Emergency Fund— which brings numbers into the conversation. My mom became a high school math teacher because she loves how math answers are either right or wrong. There is no in-between. In the same way, quantifying your goal will define it loud and clear. Numbers are far from vague.

For your emergency fund, you could open a new savings account at the bank and cut back on your eating out budget and maybe even take on extra freelance work, but you have yet to specify how you know when your goal of building an Emergency Fund is complete.

So let's quantify this goal and make $1,000 your target. Then let's quantify this goal again and set up $50 per paycheck to transfer to your new Emergency Fund account until you reach your goal.

Do you see how much easier and less overwhelming this goal sounds now that we've put a number on it? "Build a $1,000 Emergency Fund by transferring $50 per paycheck until complete" sounds much more attainable than "build an Emergency Fund."

The benefit of a clear and measurable goal is being able to clearly articulate exactly what you're shooting for—so you can celebrate when you reach it!

YOUR GOAL MUST INCLUDE A TIME-TRIGGER

The final element of an A.C.T.ual goal is a time-trigger.

You might know what you need to do to accomplish your goal, but what about when should you do it? Every day? What time of day? Should this be more of a weekly goal? Or is there a specific deadline you're shooting for?

"Someday" goals are simply not inspiring enough to get you to where you want to go. These goals exist in a state of limbo where you're not forgetting about them, but you're not actively achieving them either.

That's why every goal requires some sort of time table, whether it's a frequency or hard due date.

Some goals, like running a marathon or showcasing your new business at a local craft fair, usually have a hard deadline associated with them. Those time-triggers are easy. But for ones that don't— like organizing family photos or decluttering your home—you need to add a deadline yourself.

A deadline will encourage you to work at your goal a little every day until it's done, prioritizing what you need to do above your normal everyday tasks. There's no room for procrastination. You'll avoid delaying your goal until the very end because you know how important it is to take immediate action.

If you're afraid that setting a deadline will also set you up for failure, it's simply not true. You can always adjust! Just because life spills over our carefully time-blocked calendar boxes or unexpected events pop up or a project takes longer than you planned, doesn't mean you give up. Keep moving forward. The power is in *setting* the deadline, not meeting it perfectly.

Taking you back to my craft closet, the lack of a time-trigger was the main reason two years went by before I checked this goal off my list. I never gave it a deadline. Once I broke down my goal into smaller milestones, defined it more specifically, and told myself I had six weeks to complete one milestone, I immediately got to work. Because I had no time to lose!

Did I stick to my deadline? Not exactly.

I purchased a shelving unit and returned it a week later to try a different one. Then I had to readjust my measurements because the bins I planned to buy wouldn't fit anymore. It took me longer than I thought to sort through everything and decide what to keep versus toss. I also waffled on certain decisions, sometimes taking multiple days to make up my mind.

But I kept going. I reset my expectations and tried again.

In a matter of weeks (not years, like before!), I transformed the entire side wall of my closet into rows of ribbon, wrapping paper, and gift bags. Then I moved onto the next section and the next and the next, setting new milestone goals that were clear and actionable.

A few months later, I opened the doors to my newly organized craft closet and gazed over the neatly stacked bins and baskets that up until that point, had only existed in my mind. It was then that I finally understood the power of an A.C.T.ual goal and how important it is to apply these three elements to every goal you set.

In the following examples, you can visibly see the difference between a generic-sounding goal and one you've taken time to define.

A vague goal is: *Run a marathon*

An A.C.T.ual goal sounds more like this: Run a marathon on July 26th with a 20-week training plan that has me running 5x per week.

A vague goal is: *Build an emergency fund*

An A.C.T.ual goal sounds more like this: Save $1,000 for an emergency fund by cutting cable ($60 per month) and transferring that money to a new savings account for 16 months.

A vague goal is: *Create an organized craft closet*

An A.C.T.ual goal sounds more like this: Create an organized gift wrapping station in ⅓ of my closet by completing one task a week for six weeks.

Ahhh, much better.

Our dreams give us limitless possibilities of what *could* be. And we love the idea of molding ourselves into the person we've always envisioned. So believe me when I say I understand that the intense focus we've done together on all this preliminary planning stuff might feel... a little boring.

But remember, we're not only goal setters, we are goal *achievers*. I didn't just complete this craft closet because I had a well-defined goal. That certainly helped.

But it was the plug-and-play system I'm about to show you that allowed me to tackle my goal in a methodical, step-by-step way, with a built-in timeline. And it's going to revolutionize the way you approach goals going forward. I call it The Six-Week Sprint.

CHAPTER 5

THE SIX-WEEK SPRINT

If you can't describe what you are doing as a process, you don't know what you're doing. – W. Edwards Demming

The one buzzword I get excited about is the word systems. I spend an embarrassingly amount of time pinpointing problem areas in my home, work, and personal life, and implementing a system to solve it.

Then I tweak and retweak these *systems* on a consistent basis until they're nearly flawless. Some might say this is overkill, but I find it fun!

Unlike habits, which are triggered by a time of day or event, like washing the dishes after dinner each night, systems are a method of doing something. The HOW instead of the WHAT or WHY. If you feel like some part of your life is falling through the cracks, chances are a system would help fix it.

At one point, I noticed how much I struggled to engage with and remember what I learn from non-fiction books. There was no point in me reading these types of books if I forgot what I learned moments after I finished the final chapter.

So I spent a few days researching online to see how others remembered what they read. After taking what I thought would be helpful and leaving what I didn't, I tested my non-fiction reading system on my next book.

First, I read through the book slowly, underlining phrases and drawing a star next to important concepts. Then I added sticky flags to the pages I had just marked.

- Blue = Quotes
- Pink = Significant concept
- Orange = Studies, statistics, or stories
- Green = Action item

Since I can't add sticky flags in an eBook, I use the Kindle highlight function whenever I see something I want to remember.

When I finish the book, I open up my Growth Book (my notebook for all my notes), go through all my highlights and sticky flags and write down what I want to remember. Not only does this cement the information in my mind—there's a magical connection between your brain and physical writing versus typing—I also discover that some of the things I tabbed don't speak to me later like they did when I was reading it in the moment.

This is one of the reasons why I wait until I finish a book to make notes. I'm not writing down excess information that I don't really need *and* I don't have to juggle a book and extra notebook at the same time, which interrupts the flow of reading.

The very last step of my system is writing a review of the book. I talk about what I liked, didn't like, who this book might be for, and some key takeaways that future readers might find valuable.

I follow this system for every non-fiction book I read. And it does what I need it to—helps me retain more of what I read so I can apply that information to real life. I don't have to think about how I'm going to remember everything. I just follow the system.

That's because systems are predictable. *Repeatable*. A streamlined process to make something you do more efficient. Everything—from updating your finances to cleaning your home to achieving your goals works better when you have a system in place.

But the most popular "system" we apply to our goals isn't really a system at all.

WHY YEARLY GOALS DO MORE HARM THAN GOOD

Every year like clockwork, January 1st inspires multitudes of goal-setters to jump on social media to share their New Year intentions.

You've seen them: plans to be more present instead of scrolling mindlessly on their phone, promises to work out more instead of bingeing Netflix every evening, and even some brave souls who endeavor to complete a Whole30. Suddenly everyone wants to declutter their entire house and spend less money too.

My perfectionist personality feeds off this *newness* surrounding the first month of the year, enticing me to leave my mistakes in the past so I can start with a clean slate. I reflect on where I've been, dream about what I want to change (usually everything!), and outline, in excruciating detail, everything I want to accomplish in the next twelve months.

And yet, year after year after year, October would roll around and I'd unearth my list of goals from the pages of my planner, my cheeks burning with shame over my lack of progress. The months I had left—November and December—were some of the busiest! And there was no way I'd get it all done. So I'd stuff that paper into the garbage and wait until January 1st in hope that *next* year would be different.

Newsflash: It wasn't.

Fresh starts (like a new year, new month, or even a new day) are natural opportunities for change. But there's also a potential downside to fresh starts. Because sometimes, just the *promise* of a fresh start convinces us to put off what we could be doing now.

- Why start a fitness and healthy eating routine now when January 1st is right around the corner, after the treats of the holidays?
- Why set a new goal halfway through the month? Wouldn't it just be easier to start fresh next month? Or next year?
- Why do the laundry, clean the bathroom, or [insert whatever you're currently avoiding right now] when I can just put it off until tomorrow?

And that's when the promise of a fresh start actually turns into an excuse for a delay.

These excuses always come with a promise to change your behavior later. But as a result, you can easily fall into the "Very Last Time" mentality—I may never do (X) again, so I might as well give myself permission to indulge this one last time—usually in excess of what you would normally do.

Putting undue pressure on yourself to change everything after a certain date leads only to a self-destructive view of the way you currently think and live.

On the other hand, if you haven't made or shared your own list by that magical January 1st date, part of you feels excluded, as if your name is missing from the gold and black invitation to the year's biggest bash. You cave into the pressure of I-should-have-had-this-done-weeks ago and either set goals that don't align with your values or you throw your hands in the air and forgo setting any goals at all.

That's a lot of societal pressure to identify all our dreams and desires by the time sparkly balls drop in downtowns everywhere. But in the words of motivational author, Lara Casey, there's nothing magical about January 1st.

In fact, I think yearly goal setting does more harm than good.

It might sound nerdy to talk about brain science—this isn't a textbook, after all!—but there are two scientifically-backed reasons why yearly goals **don't** work.

The first is the Law of Diminishing Intent. This law says that the longer you wait to take action, the less likely you are to do it. We've all experienced this phenomenon at some point or another. It's why we rush into January feeling energetic and excited about all the ideas we want to do and things we want to change, then fizzle out a few months down the road.

If you stop and think about it, you've essentially given yourself twelve *long* months to work on your goal. So there's no reason to start today. Those ten pounds you want to lose don't have to come off right away. You don't need to declutter your bedroom yet. And you have all year to read twenty-five books.

But the longer you wait to start, the quicker your inspiration will fade and steal your motivation right along with it. Nothing feeds into procrastination more like the feeling you have all the time in the world to get it done.

That's why this second Law—Parkinson's Law—fits right in with the Law of Diminishing Intent. With Parkinson's Law, the time you give to a project is how long it will take.

You may have seen this play out when you block off a couple of hours to clean your entire home. And you spent all that time doing just that. But set a timer for 40 minutes and suddenly you're racing against the clock to do it in 30.

Short time-frames don't just help you get started, they are the key to following through on every goal you set.

That's what's so exciting and empowering about the plug-and-play goal-setting system I'm about to show you! Once you shift your mindset from yearly goals to shorter time-frames, you don't have to wait until January 1st. You can start whenever you want.

INTRODUCING THE SIX-WEEK SPRINT FRAMEWORK

Many people who reject the January 1st mentality try a 90-day goal setting system. Their reasoning? 90 days is long enough to make meaningful progress but also short enough to stay focused. However, I tried this 90-day method three different times. The first two were by myself. Then, hoping accountability would make a bigger difference, I partnered up with a friend for the third.

In the same fashion as my yearly goals, I started with gusto and fizzled out by week 6 or 7. I thought I had set too many goals at first, like we talked about in Chapter 3. So I narrowed it down to two. And then just one.

The results were the same.

Not only did my life and business change within those 90 days, forcing me to rethink my original goal, I also fell prey to The Law of Diminishing Intent and Parkinson's Law. I needed an even shorter timeline to maintain focus and not lose my motivation, but not so short (like a month) that I felt like I didn't have *enough* time.

And that's when I created my own goal setting system called The Six-Week Sprint. Six weeks to direct all of my energy toward one goal until I completed it, using brain science to my advantage.

The system worked.

Projects I had tried to complete as a 90-day goal with little to no progress suddenly moved off of my master to-do list and onto my finished list.

The Six-Week Sprint helped me start and finish a Dessert Recipe Binder, launch The Brainbook Printable Library (a membership site for my online business), and organize my entire book collection in the Goodreads App.

I now use it as the foundation for every goal I set.

Why is this system so successful? Just take a quick look at the benefits.

- The Six-Week Sprint System demands action right away. You have no time to procrastinate because the finish line is in sight—not twelve weeks or 52 weeks down the road.
- The shorter time-frame helps you make better decisions on what to say yes and no to. With only six weeks to work on your goal, you'll probably want to decline any new projects until your six weeks are up.
- Lastly, you won't get bored and cave into the shiny new object syndrome with The Six-Week Sprint. Every six weeks is a fresh opportunity to pursue a new goal.

The Six-Week Sprint provides the perfect blend of flexibility and structure that I find most goal-setting systems lack. As opposed to planning for a full year or even 90 days, which won't keep you laser-focused and maybe even cause you to abandon the goal entirely, with the Six-Week Sprint you'll see immediate, continued progress, week after week.

Are you ready to go deeper inside this framework and map out what your goal would look like using the Six-Week Sprint?

You should already have a well-defined A.C.T.ual goal from the last chapter—either a stand-alone goal, milestone goal, or habit goal. Ideally, this goal should take about six weeks to achieve. If not, break down your end goal into smaller, more manageable segments until you have a six-week goal.

Now it's time to plug-and-play.

1. Break down your goal into as many bite-sized action steps as possible. The worksheets found in The Six-Week Sprint Goal Planner will help you with this. Brainstorm every task needed to reach your goal in small, actionable increments.

If you envision your goal as the ultimate destination on your roadmap, we are creating all the stops along the way. Don't worry about getting everything in the right order yet. Just brain dump everything you need to do. When you're finished, look over your list and break down any big action steps even further. The smaller the action step, the more motivated you'll be to continue moving forward. I'll use my Dessert Recipe Binder as an example. When I was ready to focus on this goal, I broke it down into the following action steps:

- Buy supplies (three-ring binder and page protectors)
- Type recipes onto printable recipe cards
- Organize recipes into categories (cookies, brownies, and bars, etc.)
- Print category divider pages, recipe cards, and cover
- Make category divider tabs
- Insert into page protectors and assemble binder

Pro tip: I strongly recommend using an action verb for each step to move your task from a vague list of *things* to completable action steps. It might not seem like such a change would make that big of a difference, but your task list will feel more manageable.

Using my example above, if I just wrote down "Supplies," I wouldn't know whether to purchase the supplies or assemble them or both. Even if I needed to do both, I probably wouldn't complete both in one day. Separating out these tasks into as much detail as possible means I cross off more to-do items (yay for momentum!) and I know exactly what task I'm working on at any given moment.

2. Map out your action steps into six weekly time slots. Each week becomes a small checkpoint towards your ultimate destination—week 6. As you add each action step (or steps) to each week, keep in mind your current commitments so you don't overload one week more than another.

In my Dessert Binder example, typing recipes onto the printable recipe cards was the most time-consuming part, so I spent three of my six weeks on just that action step.

WEEK 1	WEEK 2	WEEK 3
• Buy supplies (three-ring binder and page protectors)	• Type recipes onto printable recipe cards	• Type recipes onto printable recipe cards

WEEK 4	WEEK 5	WEEK 6
• Type recipes onto printable recipe cards	• Organize categories (cookies, cake, etc) • Print divider pages, recipe cards, + cover	• Make category divider tabs • Insert into page protectors and assemble binder

The great thing about seeing all your tasks listed out like this makes it easy to shift things around based on how long a task will take, but it also motivates you to plug away at those tasks so they don't build up.

Every day and every week becomes that much more important because you only have six of them and you want to evenly space your tasks across the board. If you don't get to a task on the week you assign it, you can migrate it over to the next week (bullet journal style), but The Six Week Sprint discourages you from doing this. You don't want to overload the next week with last week's tasks and then fall behind.

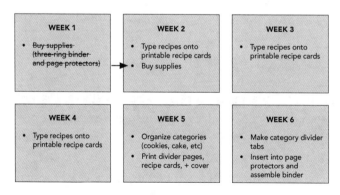

But here is the most important part. Don't let your action steps stay isolated in those weekly boxes.

3. Transfer these tasks over to whatever weekly planning system you use—whether it's a traditional paper planner or a digital app. Give space to these individual stepping stones in your weekly to-do list just like your normal, everyday tasks and make them a priority. The easiest way I find to do this is by time-blocking, using Google Calendar. I assign 1-2 hours of my week just for my Six Week Sprint. If I didn't set aside time for my own goals, then they would slip down to the bottom of my list as more pressing to-do's climbed to the top.

If you don't carve out time for what's important, then what's important won't get done. And my friend, your goals are so important!

By approaching your goals in this methodical week-by-week way, it might not feel like you're making much progress. But you'll find that the shorter focus allows you to knock out a goal faster than if you had set a yearly or a 90-day one. And when you think about it, which would you rather do? Set 10 goals for the year and finish one, maybe partially complete a second one? Or set one goal per Six Week Sprint and complete five sprints during the year?

With the latter, you'll float into December with five fully accomplished goals to your name, more than you would have if you set 10 over the next twelve months. That's because shorter timelines focus your efforts and ultimately help you be more productive.

IS THERE EVER A PLACE FOR YEARLY GOALS?

You might be wondering if there is ever a time to set yearly goals.

For some things, yes. Maybe you want to focus on a reading challenge, read through the Bible in a year, or reach a certain level of income for your side hustle.

Those are all things that align better with a yearly focus, but you still use your six-week sprints to reach them.

For instance,

- You could chop up the reading challenge to complete 1-2 books every six weeks
- You could segment your Bible reading plan to cover every six weeks instead of a year
- You could list out a number of six-week goals that would help drive income up for your business

Think long term, but when it comes down to the nitty gritty of planning, focus on the short-term action steps to see progress on those long-term results. This life-giving mindset takes the power away from the calendar cycle and puts it back into your hands. No more waiting until an arbitrary fresh start to motivate yourself again. All you need are six weeks.

CHAPTER 6

HOW TO FIND INTERNAL MOTIVATION

Motivation only has one role in our lives and that's to help us to do hard things. - Dr. BJ Fogg

Have you ever heard the quote, "Do what you love and you never have to work a day in your life"? Confucius said this.

While I love the *idea* of that phrase, I'm not sure I 100% agree.

The thing is, I enjoy weaving words and phrases together to communicate concepts in a way that are interesting and insightful. I love *having* written. But I don't always feel motivated or inspired to start the process. Writing still feels like work.

Every decision—even little ones, like the time invested in preparing a home-cooked meal versus tossing a frozen pizza in the oven—is closely tied to the motivation behind that choice.

If we are highly motivated, we may attempt a brand new recipe with thirteen steps and three ingredient-filled pans simultaneously simmering on the stovetop. If at the end of the day, our creativity and energy is shot, a frozen pizza sounds more appropriate.

We approach our goals the same way.

If we are highly motivated to follow through on our goals, the steps to achieve them won't feel so difficult. Bring it on! We're ready to crush it! But if you're not motivated at all, or your motivation fizzles out after a few weeks, the path suddenly seems rocky, steep, and littered with distractions.

In short, motivation not only drives our behavior, it also drives the level of enthusiasm *behind* that behavior.

So where does motivation come from? And more importantly, how can you harness the power of motivation to support your goals from beginning to end?

By first understanding the two types of motivation—internal motivation (also called intrinsic motivation) and external motivation (or extrinsic motivation) and secondly, how each type of motivation plays into your big-picture goal.

Internal motivation comes from within. You are motivated to achieve your goal based on your own thoughts, feelings, and personal values. This is one of the reasons why it's essential to set goals that align with your values. If your goal does not have personal significance, the motivation will quickly fade... if you started with any at all.

Examples of internal motivation would be:

- Learning to speak Spanish because you want to develop a new skill, not because your new job requires it.
- Starting a fitness program because you enjoy the way exercising makes you feel, not because you want to fit into a smaller size dress for your cousin's wedding.
- Writing for the pure satisfaction of the end result rather than meeting a deadline.

External motivation stems from outside influences. There is either the promise of an external reward (or punishment), recognition and praise from others, or pressure resulting from a factor outside your control.

Examples of external motivation would be:

- A child who cleans their room because a parent has threatened a consequence if they do otherwise.
- Performing routine tasks at work in exchange for a paycheck.
- Athletes who adopt a rigorous training program in order to compete at the Olympics.

The difference lies in whether your motivation comes from outside yourself or from within. Both can be extremely helpful when reaching a goal, but I would argue that a strong internal motivation is the foundation to every goal you set...and the first place you should start.

FIND YOUR WHY

Simon Sinek has given one of the most famous speeches in Ted Talks history—"Start With Why," which he later transformed into a best-selling book.

His premise? People don't follow what you do; they follow *why* you do it. While he gears his speech more toward business leaders (like why Apple products cultivate such a cult following), the same principle applies to every one of our goals, be it as big as writing a book or as small as starting a journaling habit.

Knowing WHAT you want to do won't pull you out of bed in the morning. Not by a long shot. Knowing your WHY will.

I'm sure you've felt this way as you lie in bed vacillating whether or not to hit snooze again (which feels good in the moment) rather than getting up and turning on your workout video (which doesn't feel worth it when you're exhausted!).

That's because as humans, we subconsciously evaluate everything we do with a measuring stick of pleasure versus pain. And we want to avoid pain as much as possible. Only if the pleasure of something outweighs the pain you need to go through to do it will you find a way to make it happen.

I'll share a personal example of this.

One Friday (the day I always update my finances), I saw vivid red numbers glaring at me from the brightly lit screen of my budgeting app. We went over on groceries... again. This was three months in a row now. I wish I could say we crossed our self-imposed limit by only a few dollars, but we spent $50-$80 more than what we had originally planned.

So I began to justify the expense. We hosted Joseph's birthday with enough food to feed 10 people. That seemed like a good excuse. Or we were RVing in a rural area where grocery stores charged double the price of what we normally expect to pay.

I combed through my mental checklist of all the reasons why this wasn't a big deal (I could just cover the overage from another budget category after all).

The truth was, neither Joseph nor I had a compelling reason to stay under our budget besides "that's what financially savvy people *should do.*" For some ultra-disciplined personalities, that internal pep talk might be enough. But for us, the "right thing" did nothing to help us avoid the negative numbers in our grocery budget at the end of the month.

So after another few months of extra spending and frustration, we looked over the budget sheet and made a pact that enough was enough. And we did something we had never done before.

We established our WHY.

We decided that any extra money we had leftover in our grocery budget would go towards our retirement account. As two self-employed individuals, we don't have the luxury of a company 401K.

So, any time we came in under budget, we wouldn't drive to the nearest grocery store and load up on snacks to use every last penny. We would transfer that extra money over to our retirement account. By having a WHY, we were able to give ourselves a reason beyond "it feels like the right thing to do." We could literally visualize our results in the form of money left over in that line item of our budget.

The first month that we followed through on our pact, we came in $20 under budget. That $20 might not seem like a lot, but add up $20 over a year or two, and the end result makes each month feel like a significant difference. By year's end, that's an extra $240! Not to mention we spent less than the three months previous because now we weren't just under budget, we weren't going over budget any longer.

There's nothing wrong with writing all the motivating mantras you want on sticky notes and sticking them on your bathroom mirror, but our willingness to follow through on our goals often boils down to why we want to reach them.

So anytime you set a new goal, take the necessary steps to ask yourself:

1. Why do YOU want to achieve this goal? Not why you think you should, but what you're hoping to get after putting in all the effort.
2. Why should you put your time and energy into this goal over something else you could be doing?
3. Why will this goal make your life better, easier, and more fulfilling?

These questions will help you pinpoint the purpose behind every goal you set. It's also why I don't want you to skip your WHY section in your Six-Week Sprint Goal Planner.

This section will help you establish a reason (or multiple reasons) that speak powerfully and personally to you. Once you've written this down, review your WHY as often as it takes to make it stick. Your why will keep the big picture in mind when motivation decides to take a back seat and you're tempted to give up on your goal.

You won't avoid hard days completely (all journeys come with ups and downs), but you'll remember what you're doing it all for. And this knowledge will make those hard days a little easier.

So will adding this next tool to your motivational toolkit.

PAY ATTENTION TO YOUR ENERGY

In the middle of writing this book, I asked my Instagram community a fundamental question.

"What is the biggest obstacle that keeps you from reaching your goals?"

The word that kept popping up as I scrolled through the comments was...TIME. Oh how we wish we had more of it!

People had the hardest time *finding time* to complete their goals. And when they did have an extra moment to spare, they overestimated how much they could accomplish in that time frame, leaving them drained, discouraged, and unmotivated.

This may be hard to hear, but you can micromanage every minute of your day and still fall short. I don't want this statement to discourage you. I want it to free you. There is simply not enough hours in a day for you to realistically be productive 100% of the time.

You can download a new app, try to become more organized, shave minutes off your time by creating a 5-minute makeup routine or ordering grocery pickup. Unexpected things will still happen. And you're not a robot who can mindlessly pivot from one thing to the next.

So while on the surface, better time management may solve a few things, I find that what makes the biggest difference is knowing how to manage your energy *so you can better manage your time.*

Energy ebbs and flows. Unlike time, which is consistent every minute, 24 hours a day, there are small windows during the day when your energy is high and low. If you're a morning person, you already know this. By 8pm, you're probably starting to fade, right when night owls are most alert.

Better energy management starts when you identify those peak hours of high energy and use that window to your advantage. This window is where you'll find the energy to work consistently on your goals and with the least resistance.

It's funny, but I don't consider myself a morning or night person. When I track my mood throughout the day, I find that my peak hours are between 9am-12pm. This is past my initial morning grogginess but before the afternoon slump. Then I'll get a small burst of energy right after dinner—usually around 7pm—that will last about an hour.

During the 9am-12pm window, I schedule one action step that brings me closer to my goal. I don't use the entire three hours (although that would be lovely!). Instead, I carve out one hour during that time frame where I "go dark." I put my phone on Do Not Disturb, let Joseph know I'm about to enter the "zone", and focus 100% on my goal for the next 60 minutes.

I call this my Tiger Time.

Amy Porterfield[1] coined this term to illustrate how fiercely you should protect this time—like a mama tiger would her cub. That's how you should feel about your goals. Carve out time to work on them and protect that time at all costs. That's why I block out time for my goals on my Google Calendar. I'm more likely to stick to my plan when it looks like an appointment.

So if you want to make progress on your goals with a good amount of energy, you need to find your Tiger Time.

Think through your day and notice the times when your energy feels a little higher. Notice when it's low. Then plan accordingly. Don't fill that time with activities that drain you—like making a phone call or answering emails or cleaning the bathroom. I'm sure you have a mental list! Instead, fill that time with work that requires the most focus: your goals.

I love how Carey Nieuwhof, leadership author, puts it. "You'll be able to do twice the amount of your best work because you're doing it when you're at your best."

That's because when you focus on time management, you think about how much you can pack into a day. But when you focus on energy management, you strip away all the should-do's and zero in on the things you actually need to do. You don't push yourself past the point of exhaustion.

ACT HOW YOU WANT TO FEEL

Perhaps you're thinking this sounds great for people wired with a high-capacity personality. People who thrive on being busy with their go-go-go mentality to keep them moving throughout the day.

But for others, like me (and possibly you, too), who struggle with depression, anxiety, and other health concerns that involve side effects like chronic fatigue, you know what it's like to swim against the current when you attempt normal everyday tasks. Sometimes taking a shower can feel like a big chore! But that may just be me wanting to avoid the upcoming workout required to dry and style my thick, frizzy hair. Ha!

Obviously, I don't want to downplay those days when your energy battery needs an extra charge. We have to take breaks. Rest is good... and important. Far too often, we overschedule ourselves to the point of exhaustion, and I'll be the first to tell you not to sacrifice self-care.

But if you've taken time to rest and still feel unmotivated, it's time to fake it until you make it. You can't tie your success to willpower alone. You must *act* how you want to *feel*.

American social scientist BJ Fogg[2] has done extensive research on motivation and concluded that motivation comes in waves. Seems obvious based on what we've already discussed, doesn't it? That's why we feel so excited at the beginning of the new year or a new goal. Or when we see someone doing the same thing we'd like to do. Or we read something inspiring. We're riding a wave!

But waves don't stay the same. They rise and fall. Just like motivation. Just like your energy.

When we rely on feelings (or the high point of a wave) to dictate our actions, we're setting ourselves up for major disappointment.

For me, I don't always feel like working out or reading a nonfiction book, or making dinner, for that matter. I'm sure you can think of multiple examples in your own life when you've mumbled, "I just don't feel like it."

And sometimes, you give in. You don't do what you don't feel.

But when you push past that uncomfortable feeling and take action anyway, something magical happens. You develop that motivation. The wave trends upward again. All it takes is that initial start.

If you need to, you can even tell yourself you'll just give this task five minutes—no matter what you're trying to avoid. I often use this hack when I sit down to write and have no creative energy to come up with any words.

I tell myself, *just write for five minutes.* After those five minutes, I can stop. But what usually happens is I'm in the flow of things so much that I can't stop. Even if they are terrible words, they flow from my fingertips for another 45-50 minutes, when I'm finally ready for a break.

So the next time your feelings don't match up with the action you need to take, fake it. Push yourself. Act how you want to feel. It won't take long for your feelings to change.

And if not, I have one more secret for you in the next chapter.

CHAPTER 7

HOW TO HARNESS EXTERNAL MOTIVATION

Commitment is what transforms a promise into reality.
- Abraham Lincoln

Have you ever heard of The Marshmallow Experiment?[9]

In the 1960s, a Stanford professor named Walter Mischel began a series of studies with 4- and 5-year-old children and he used... you guessed it. Marshmallows.

These children were led one-by-one to a private room and left alone with one marshmallow for 15-20 minutes. They were told if they did not eat that marshmallow, the researcher would offer them another one when he returned. Then they could have two marshmallows!

This simple choice—eat one treat now or get two later—had different reactions depending on the child.

Some ate the marshmallow right away. Others tried to resist temptation by wiggling in their chairs, scooting around, and probably picking their noses (they *were* only 4 and 5!) to distract themselves. But eventually, most of them gave in. Notice I said most. Not all.

There were a handful of children who successfully waited. When their time was up, the researcher returned to the room and rewarded them with their promised marshmallow.

Years later, other researchers followed up with the children who had originally resisted their marshmallow-eating impulses. And they made a startling discovery. These children ended up having higher SAT scores, better social skills, and were successful in multiple areas of their life.

You could argue that internal motivation (in this case, represented by delayed gratification), allowed these children to demonstrate significant willpower to wait. But they didn't exclusively rely on their internal drive to prove to themselves that they were capable of resisting temptation.

They were promised a reward if they waited. An *external* motivator. And that promise helped them follow through.

The truth is, sometimes we need outside help. As much as we try to remember our WHY, as much as we try to manage our energy and work on our goals during the most alert times of our day, our internal drive doesn't always deliver.

Researchers will argue against this, saying that internal motivation is the preferred method to reach your goals. It's true. Internal motivation does offer a more meaningful connection. If you love your job because of *what* you do versus clocking in just for the paycheck, you'll be a happier person (and a happier employee and co-worker) overall.

But when you leverage a balance of both, as I recommend doing here, you influence your behavior with a powerhouse of motivational tools—both internally and externally based.

So start with internal motivation. Dig deep inside yourself to figure out what will fuel you to reach this goal as we explored in the last chapter. Then tap into external motivation as an extra boost to follow through.

External motivation—as we'll discover through the power of accountability and rewards—will propel you forward when that internal motivation isn't quite as strong or starts to fade.

DEPEND ON AN OUTSIDE SOURCE

So far, the only person holding you responsible for your goals is you. And that may be all you need... or want.

But relationships exist for a reason—we thrive in community! The 2020 pandemic took a massive toll on our mental health because we couldn't see friends and extended family for months. Some didn't see their loved ones for over a year. As much as we tried to adapt, screens can't replace the warmth of a hug or the heart behind face-to-face conversations.

So if community is important, why wouldn't we take advantage of our community to reach a goal, which is also important? Accountability plays a crucial role in our success.

I'll be honest—I used to hate the idea of accountability (total introvert here). Failing is one thing, but failing in front of someone else? That's an open invitation for judgment. No thanks.

That is, until I tried my own accountability experiment.

For months, I had been following the same workout videos every day... and I was tired of it. I needed to switch up my workout schedule or I risked not working out at all. So I found a 30-day plank challenge on Pinterest and printed a paper copy to paste inside my bullet journal. The goal was to increase my plank time every week until I could do a five-minute plank.

Except the 30 days didn't go quite as planned.

One skipped day turned into two, then three, and sometimes four. By the time I started up again, I felt like I had made no progress at all.

So I tried again. But this time, I took the challenge to social media. I made a pact to check in everyday on Instagram stories to show a photo of me doing a plank, or my bullet journal, or workout clothes—something inspiring that communicated to my community that I was committed to this challenge.

And it worked—go figure! I still missed a few days here and there (perfection wasn't the point), but I felt pretty proud of myself when I finished that five-minute plank and checked off Day 30. I could have never done that without the pressure I put on myself to share this journey with my community.

My experience isn't an anomaly. People much smarter than me at The American Society of Training and Development[10] found that if you have a specific accountability appointment with someone, you will increase your chance of success up to 95%. Read that again. How would you like to give yourself a 95% chance of success? That's incredible!

Isn't it funny how we're driven by others' expectations, sometimes more than our own?

We can make all the excuses in the world as to why we don't do something. It's easier to give in or give up when only our personal pride is on the line. But when someone else is involved? When someone else knows what we've committed to and we don't do it?

Suddenly, we are too embarrassed to phone it in.

Use this knowledge to your advantage. Ask a friend if she wants to go walking with you. Set up a text string of accountability partners who want to read their Bible every day. Start a blog or an Instagram account or a Facebook group. Share your progress with others so you won't be tempted to quit.

With the right support, you can achieve any goal you set. And the likelihood of that happening is higher when you report your progress to someone else...and they hold your feet to the fire.

However, there's more than one way to apply accountability. A friend or family member acting as your "check-in" for the day isn't the only accountability tool at your disposal. If you are motivated by *personal* accountability, you can try Seinfield's "Don't Break the Chain" strategy.[11]

When Jerry Seinfield created a goal to write new material for his stand-up comedy routine, he hung a big calendar on his wall and wrote a large red "X" on each day he succeeded. Drawing those X's were pretty rewarding in themselves, so he kept doing it. His only goal was to not break the chain.

This strategy is especially helpful when you are working on a habit-based goal. Maybe you've thought of an activity you want to do every day, whether it's journaling, drinking eight glasses of water, reading for 20 minutes, or something else you want to practice on a consistent basis.

Choose an accountability tool where you can track concrete and visible *daily* progress. You can use a big wall calendar like Jerry Seinfeld, draw a simple habit tracker in your bullet journal, or download a habit-tracking app if you prefer digital tracking.

Here's why this works: You don't have to focus on what happens a few days from now. You can just do what you need to today. And with every win—with every "X" or checkmark—you'll hit that stride where your habit becomes easier and easier to start.

When you introduce accountability into your goals, you don't just prove to others that your goal is a priority, you prove it to yourself. If you don't share your goals in some way, are you really committing to them? Do they exist outside your mind? Are they tangible?

Accountability provides an extra layer of support for your goal. Meanwhile, rewards provide an extra incentive.

VALIDATE YOUR HARD WORK

If you browse the app store for just a few minutes, you'll find dozens of companies who promise cash or gift cards if you complete specific tasks. Sometimes, you need to shop through their app. Others might require photos of your receipts or ask you to take a short survey.

You probably already have a few of these apps downloaded on your phone. I have four!

But apps are not the only source of extra perks. Credit card rewards offer 1%-5% cash back on select purchases. Hotel programs reward you with a free night based on how many points you earn on each stay. Grocery store loyalty cards take a few cents off your gas purchase depending on how much you've spent with them in a certain period of time.

Even ice cream shops will punch a small card when you order a treat. After ten punches, you get one scoop of free ice cream in a cone or dish.

So many businesses offer rewards now that we are programmed to expect them. And why?

Well, rewards work.

When you order a $25 gift card for uploading receipts or redeem a free hotel night or receive a punch on your loyalty card, there's a dopamine spike in your brain. You earned a reward! That dopamine effect inspires you to do it all over again. The reward just proved to you that your efforts (big or small) are worth continuing.

It's why attaching a reward to our goals is so powerful. They deliver the same feel-good response.

If you're struggling to adopt a new lifestyle change or you're attempting a goal that scares you a little bit, rewards add a fun incentive in exchange for the behavior you want to see. There's nothing wrong with bribing yourself toward success—either by sprinkling in small, motivating rewards along the way or holding out for one big reward at the end. Or both!

And every time you collect that well-deserved reward, your brain says, "WAY TO GO! When can we do this again?!" You can't fake that level of satisfaction.

Some people don't need this kind of recognition or incentive. Their dopamine levels fare just fine because they see their completed goal *as* the reward. And you should be thrilled (obviously!) with what you accomplish. But I'm also encouraging you to celebrate in an extra special way. Because an additional reward on top of that goal you just crushed?

That's icing on the proverbial goal-achieving cake.

And it's a sure-fire way to spike that dopamine even higher.

As you're considering which rewards to choose, keep two things in mind: 1) Focus on rewards that keep you motivated without sabotaging your actual goal and 2) always follow through with the reward. The latter sounds like it shouldn't be a problem—of course you'll redeem your reward! But I'll explain why the finish line tempts us to skip them in a minute.

For now, I want you to recognize that reward setting is just as personal as goal setting. If you treat yourself to something you don't really care about, you're not going to shout, "Yes! I made it! I want to keep going!" You can't follow what other people use as rewards for their goals and expect it to work. Instead, think of what rewards would motivate you. What would you love to receive as a gift?

For example, if you hate shopping for new clothes, picking out a new dress after completing a 30-day fitness plan probably won't inspire you to work out. But you know what might? A new book if you're an avid reader. Or a fun water bottle. Even the promise of a Target gift card can give you a boost if you always leave that store with a cart full of items you didn't need but bought anyway. (Of which I'm guilty!)

Bottom line: there's no point in setting a reward if you don't look forward to earning it.

But just as rewards need to be motivating to you, they also shouldn't derail your goals—especially when meeting a fitness or savings goal. If you're trying to lose weight, eating a candy bar after every workout probably isn't a good idea. Neither would saving $100 a month only to spend $80 on a massage.

There is a balance here.

Just make sure that you do reward yourself. Because one time, I almost didn't. And I soon realized that without a reward, I was careening headfirst toward burnout.

A few years ago, before I developed The Six-Week Sprint, I set a Q1 sales goal and told myself I could go get a pedicure (my guilty pleasure) when I crushed it. I worked extra hard on an email campaign, knowing that the outcome of this campaign would determine whether or not I indulged in pretty pink toes.

At the end of the three months, I totaled up the amounts and discovered that I had surpassed my goal. With a wide grin, I shared my win with Joseph and we celebrated with high-fives and hugs for a few minutes.

And then it was over. A few weeks later, I still hadn't made my pedicure appointment and wasn't sure I was even going to. I was so focused on my next goal—my next mountain to conquer—that my reward didn't seem so significant anymore.

But what's the use of goal-setting if you can't enjoy the sense of achievement that comes with completing it? Adding a reward (especially one you look forward to) means that yes, you're more likely to give that goal everything you've got. But it also gives you an excuse to celebrate what you've already done.

Motivation builds when we appreciate how far we've come rather than focus on how far we have to go.

In the end, Joseph strongly encouraged me to call and schedule my appointment. And I'm so glad I did. Because I enjoyed every minute of my pedicure!

As I sat in the massage chair with water bubbling around my ankles, I finally understood how much our bodies crave (and deserve) validation for our hard work. When we quickly move onto the next thing without fully reflecting on our achievements, we cheapen the effort and struggle it took to get there.

I want you to honor yourself—and honor your goal—by valuing the payoff.

MAKE SUCCESS RIDICULOUSLY EASY

In season three of the medical drama called *The Resident*, a plastic surgeon (named Dr. Wong) has the monumental task of doing a double hand transplant for a young boy. In the hours before any big operation, almost every surgeon in this fictional TV hospital has a pre-surgical routine. Some listen to music while others double- and triple-check that they have every tool they need.

But the surgeons were surprised to hear Dr. Wong's routine from outside the Operating Room. He was verbally reciting a list of *everything* that could go wrong. What a way to begin a surgery!

However, because he took time to think through every worst case scenario, he was adequately prepared when something *did* go wrong in his operating room. He had the foresight to plan ahead and ready the solution ahead of time.

Now I realize this is a TV show. Maybe real surgeons don't even have these types of routines. I don't know. The point is, you'll probably encounter a few obstacles along your goal-achieving path.

But when you take the time to prepare for these obstacles before you even start, you'll be better equipped to respond when they appear.

This is why I created a section in The Six-Week Sprint Goal Planner to record any obstacles you might face when trying to reach your goal. It could be timing. Lack of energy. Other tasks getting in the way. Or because you're afraid of failing and your insecurity keeps you paralyzed in fear.

I don't want you to be surprised when an obstacle rears its ugly head, which is why it's important to list them. List everything that could potentially derail you from making progress on your goal.

I understand that it might feel a little discouraging (and weird) to see all these challenges listed right next to the one thing you want most. That's one way to destroy all the excitement, thanks! But as Michael Hyatt says in his book, Your Best Year Ever, "Create contingencies when you are at your strongest, rather than relying on your willpower when you're not."

You've already learned that your willpower battery doesn't stay fully charged. That's why it's better to come up with a contingency plan when your battery is at 100% rather than hitting a snag at 28% and then deciding how you want to overcome this bump in the road.

"Decision fatigue" is real.

If you're not familiar with this concept, decision fatigue works like this: We all have a max number of decisions we can make each day... and make WELL. When you've reached your max, your brain starts spinning and your ability to think strategically disappears.

So when you pick and choose certain things that are the same each day, you don't waste precious brain power making a decision about it. And when you streamline decision-making in your daily life, you have more time and energy to do the things you actually want to do.

This is why capsule wardrobes are so popular. I have one... kind of. While I haven't invested in tops and bottoms that seamlessly mix and match, I try to stay within the same color scheme—light pinks and mauves, blues, and neutrals. Absolutely no yellows, reds, or purples.

Some colors I just don't like. Others look horrible with my skin color! However, because I don't hem and haw over my closet each day, wondering what to wear and what to wear together, I'm saving time and energy, thus eliminating decision fatigue. My minimalist wardrobe also saves me time at the store. I go straight to the colors and styles I know will look good and skip the rest.

You have to expect that multiple decision-making opportunities will show up as you pursue your goals. So take some time *ahead* of time to brainstorm potential solutions for each decision or obstacle you might face as you work towards your goal. These solutions should make it ridiculously easy for your future self to do the right thing.

They could be as simple as:

- Automatic transfers from your checking account to your savings so you don't have to think about making the transfer on a busy payday... and possibly forgetting to do it.
- Choosing your workout clothes the night before and setting them right where you'll see them when you wake up. You'll face one less obstacle (and decision) before turning on your workout video.
- Deleting a social media app after a certain time of day so you're not tempted to open it back up when you're bored.

Don't let your brain trick you into giving up; trick your brain into thinking it doesn't have to work so hard. Pave the smoothest path possible for yourself so you can't help but succeed. And when you hit those pesky roadblocks, you'll know what to do. You've already done the heavy lifting.

CHAPTER 8

LIVE A LIFE WITHOUT REGRETS

Twenty years from now you will be more disappointed by the things that you didn't do than by the ones you did do. - Mark Twain

I never thought I'd spend Easter Sunday huddled in a women's shower stall.

We were camping in a state park in Alabama when we saw a big storm system moving through the south, leaving dozens of tornado touchdowns in its wake. We knew we might need to evacuate. So we prepped all morning and afternoon just in case we needed to find shelter.

We readied the bunny carrier, tied down items that could potentially fly away, and stashed all our devices in Joseph's laptop bag so we could grab our essentials and go.

When that tornado warning boomed from our weather radio, we scooped up the bunnies and dashed to the closest concrete structure—the RV camp bathhouse—and spent the next 45 minutes glued to our phones streaming live coverage of the storm.

The tornado missed us (thankfully!) and whirled through a town 8 miles south of us. Still too close for comfort, but we were safe. Our RV was intact. We had so much to be grateful for! Throughout the entire event, two things kept us from panicking.

1. Prayers from our family and friends.
2. The calm, measured voice of a local meteorologist.

He communicated the seriousness of what was going on without the hysteria that often defines dramatic events, especially on social media. He told us what areas needed to find shelter and where we had the all-clear. His career experience covering hundreds of storms earned our trust.

He also said something that stuck with me long after the storm was gone. It was meant for people living in areas *without* the tornado warning, but still close enough to be affected.

"Choose the path of *least* regret."

In other words, if you would feel safer moving to a room without windows or evacuating to an area shelter, go. Make the decision that offers the least amount of regret if a tornado were to appear.

This phrase is especially helpful to remember when waffling between hard decisions. Is it time to change careers? What type of schooling is best for your kids? Should you move back home to take care of your parents or help them find a place closer to you?

These are tough decisions! When you're faced with any significant life change, most of us would rather step back and worry about the potential negatives of each choice, rather than step forward in confidence and commit. We don't want to experience regret.

But choosing the path of least regret doesn't have to eliminate regret entirely. There's no one perfect choice that can. Unfortunately, it doesn't matter which path you choose; you will probably give up something either way.

Changing careers might mean less time at home but more financial stability. Homeschooling your kids will give them a more personalized experience, but they might not have the opportunity to participate in organized sports. Moving closer to your parents would uproot you from your community. But moving your parents would uproot them from theirs.

Neither choice is wrong. The focus here is least regret. Which trade-off are you willing to take?

You don't have to time-travel very far to find out what your future self would say. Because when you look at your current life through the lens of an older, wiser version of yourself—whether it's a few hours from now or a few years from now—you've added another tool (perspective) to make a more *informed* choice.

And you can avoid being the person who wished they had made a different one.

THE UNIVERSAL NATURE OF REGRET

In 2009, Bronnie Ware published an online article titled *The Top 5 Regrets of the Dying*.[1] She worked in palliative care, spending time with patients who only had 3-12 weeks to live. I can't help but think how strong she had to be to walk into work every day knowing the unchangeable outcome of every patient.

Most of us don't want to think about death, but Bronnie had a front row seat to those who faced that terrifying possibility every day. And even though they each had vastly different experiences and backgrounds, there was one common thread.

Regret.

As people reflected on their lives, they wished they could have been more genuine—able to express their feelings without fear of judgment, instead of living a life others expected of them.

They wished they hadn't worked so hard or had made more of

an effort to stay in touch with friends instead of letting those once-important relationships fade away.

Most of all, they regretted not letting themselves be happier. Their pursuit of more did not bring the contentment they longed for. And with everything stripped away, as they faced death at any moment, they wished they could have enjoyed simple pleasures that made them laugh and smile versus always working towards financial gain.

I know this is heavy. We don't want to imagine ourselves in their shoes, with nothing to do but think over all the ways you could have lived your life differently.

But if we understand that regret stems from a dissonance between what you want your life to look like and what it actually is, we'll take positive steps forward to create a past we're proud of.

Regret is a powerful motivator.

In fact, understanding the power of regret was what finally convinced both Joseph and I to take the leap into full-time RV living. We knew every day wouldn't be glamorous. The nights we sit by the campfire and watch the sky turn orange as the sun dips below majestic canyon features are lovely.

But we don't experience them all the time.

Just a few weeks ago, we scrambled into a Cracker Barrel parking lot as the sky turned to dusk. Our previous three campsites had fallen through and we had nowhere else to go. Talk about feeling homeless when you literally take your home with you!

When I laid down to sleep that night, eyes throbbing from the bright streetlight just outside our window, my brain took a trip back in time. I remembered the day we decided to sell our sticks-and-bricks home, and I wondered if we had done the right thing.

That home felt safe. I didn't have to worry about finding a location for it or getting a knock at 3am telling us to move. That home stayed right where it was built.

But unlike that home, I didn't want to stay in the same place forever. Because my greatest regret would be to play it safe and miss out on all the unique experiences that changed weekly outside our front door.

The truth is, we're not going to make the right decisions every time. That's not only impossible, it's unrealistic. And it's good to learn from our mistakes. Franklin D. Roosevelt said, "A smooth sea never made a skilled sailor." What is there to learn if life is going great?

So don't let this one experience fool you into thinking I don't have any regrets. I've regretted plenty, just as I'm sure you have.

The secret? Don't let regret keep you stuck over decisions you made in the past. Turn what you wish you *had* done into what you're *going* to do now.

UNDERSTAND WHAT'S AT STAKE

As human beings, our brains are twice as sensitive to what can go wrong as to what might go right.

We see this concept play out in the news. When Joseph worked as a cameraman for a local news station, reporters pitched significantly more negative stories in their morning meetings than positive ones. You can't turn off the television when you hear the next segment is about how you're being scammed or the "3 Things Your Doctor Won't Tell You."

Fear sells.

I wish I could argue against this, but the data backs it up. We feel more pain over losing $100 than excitement over gaining $100. It's why at the end of people's lives, they regret more of the risks they didn't take than those they did.

While there is a time and place to focus on the positive end of our

WHY, like we did in chapter 6, we can still use negative angles to our advantage. Because the negative consequences are the ones that will actually light a fire under us. They are what keep us moving forward even when we don't feel like taking action at all.

And to do that, we need to know what's at stake if we don't reach our goal.

We've all experienced that devastating realization the moment we realize we're not going to make our goal. Real life happens. You have to pivot sometimes, whether it's by changing the goal or changing your approach *to* a goal.

But there could be other reasons too. Maybe you procrastinated too long. Or you didn't carve out specific (or enough) time on your calendar to make steady progress.

Whatever your reasoning, you need to have a legitimate stake in the outcome so you don't walk away as easily. You must fully understand what you stand to lose.

Growing up, I attended a private Christian school K-12, where I became intimately aware of the rules and consequences of not following those rules. You could get a warning. Then demerits. Then detention if you acted really terrible.

In first grade, a friend and I thought it was a good idea to draw on the gymnasium bleachers. Not just draw... *carve our names.* Real smart.

It didn't take long before we heard those same names called over the loudspeaker. The principal summoned us to his office where we stood, wide-eyed and hands behind our backs as we tried to explain away our behavior.

But our excuses didn't work. For the next hour, we scrubbed not just our pen marks out of the bleachers, but every blemish we could find.

This big cleaning session was our (well-deserved) punishment.

But you know what hurt more than scrubbing bleachers? What made me reflect long and hard about what I had done? The fact that I had disappointed someone else.

The knowledge that I had let others down was what ultimately changed my behavior. I never defaced property again.

That's the reality of behavior change. It connects to a deeper part of you. So if you want to know what's really at stake if you don't reach a goal, you need to peel back the top layer and find the true consequence underneath, then use that consequence to drive your behavior.

You need to have some skin in the game if you want to *win* the game.

Thinking back to the external motivators from the last chapter, here are a few "top layer" things that could happen if you don't reach your goal:

- You might not redeem your reward.
- You might feel embarrassed that you didn't check in with an accountability partner.
- You could be disappointed that you didn't put an "X" in your habit tracker. Those aren't fun for a perfectionist, especially leaving blank spaces in a habit tracker—I'll be the first to admit it!

But in the end, none of those things mean all that much. Not when you figure out what is *really* at stake. Because the answer to that question will bring you back full circle to why you wanted to achieve this goal in the first place.

Let's say that one of your Six-Week Sprint goals is to organize your digital photos. Right now your photos are everywhere—they're located on your phone, your spouse's phone, that fancy DSLR camera that you still don't know how to use, and on social media from friends who took photos of you and/or your family, but you don't yet have a copy.

So you break down all of your action steps, week-by-week, from researching photo back-up options to creating an ongoing system that will keep your photos organized long-term.

But one week goes by, then two, then six and you've finished *some* tasks toward your goal, but not all. Then a few months later after you've abandoned this goal entirely, your desktop computer fails. The hard drive crashes and all the photos you have are gone because you didn't get a chance to back them up to an external cloud.

This exact scenario happened to me. I'll never be able to recover those photos from our Key West vacation, among others. I was devastated to lose them!

My memories were at stake. My consequence was losing them.

For others, what's at stake could be entirely different, but no less painful.

Not building an Emergency Fund could lead to an unexpected expense completely devastating your finances. Spending too much time at night on your phone could result in severe sleep deprivation the next morning. Putting off the vacation you always envisioned might mean never going at all because of an unexpected diagnosis.

When you define what's at stake, when you think through everything that could happen if you don't achieve this goal, you automatically increase your *ability* to achieve it. Negative reinforcement isn't my first choice either. But oh how it works!

And acknowledging this discomfort is so much better than ignoring it entirely.

CHANGE YOUR NORMAL

As we close, I want to share one more concept that will forever change the way you view your goals.

We've all seen the effects of lifestyle inflation. When your income level rises, your spending gradually increases to meet it. One raise here, a bonus check there, and suddenly, you have an extra $200-$500 (or more) to buy nicer clothes or add another streaming subscription or invest in a better car or maybe even an additional car.

Things that were once luxuries become necessities. They change your normal.

But while lifestyle inflation isn't celebrated in the financial world, there are some positive aspects we can apply to our goals. James Clear, author of *Atomic Habits*, argues that if you can change your normal everyday routines to be in line with your goals, your results will follow.

It makes sense.

Waking up earlier would give you more time to fit in a workout. Establishing a reading routine would help you plow you through more books. Studying a new language for 15 minutes a day would move you closer to becoming fluent.

When you integrate these things into a routine you already have, or establish a new routine to accommodate them, you gradually rise to the level of that routine. Achieving your goal becomes your new normal.

I want to make goal-setting normal. Not this one-off thing you do around January 1st or when you're suddenly inspired by what someone else has achieved. Or because you feel guilty for all the things you haven't done yet and want to.

No. I want goal setting and goal achieving to become second nature to you. I want it to be something you make progress toward every day. I want you to see success after success after success so that one goal snowballs into ten, which snowballs into twenty and beyond. And after celebrating what you've achieved, you're ready to go at it again.

Because now you know exactly what to do.

You know why goals are important, how to define your core values, why you should narrow down your list of goals to *just* one (for now at least!), what it means to create an A.C.T.ual goal, the best system to use to reach your goal, and how to stay motivated long-term.

We've covered a lot in the previous chapters together! I'm so glad you stuck with me. I'm proud of you for making it this far and doing the hard work of goal-achieving. As you've discovered, this is so much more than just goal-setting. There are a lot of factors at play that will help you follow through to the very end.

That is what I wish for you. To see consistent, sustainable change that lasts. To change your normal.

So will you join me? Together, we can show the world that it's normal to achieve your dreams. We are practical dreamers, after all.

ACKNOWLEDGMENTS

Joseph: There's no achievement in my life that doesn't include you. From cake baking in the early days to taking photos of me for Instagram, I see every success as our success because of your dedicated support behind-the-scenes. There were many times during this process when I wanted to give up. You patiently listened while I talked through each "problem area" helping me solve what I wanted to change but didn't always know how to communicate. Thank you for always having my back. Love you always!

Rachelle: From the very beginning, you've believed in this message and you believed in me. Whether I rewrote entire chapters or moved sections around or you edited the same paragraph five different times, you never made me feel like an inconvenience. Your thoughtfulness and attention to detail helped me feel confident enough to send this book into the world. Thank you for caring about this message as if it were your own!

Melissa: What a treat it has been to have you on board this year! You jumped right into this project without hesitation, even learning a new program so you could beautifully package the words inside this book. I'm forever in awe of your design expertise and your eagerness to help uncover my vision.

Melinda: I could not have written this book were it not for your continued work behind the scenes, taking care of administrative tasks so I could dedicate large time blocks to writing. Thank you for making sure everyone you communicate with feels valued and understood. Your willingness to be a second pair of eyes on my draft meant the world to me!

Lauren and Michelle: Our virtual meetings (and occasional in-person meetings!) are the bright spots in my week. What started out as a business-focused mastermind turned into a long-lasting friendship with two incredible women. You both encouraged me to tackle this topic even though I lamented this was the hardest thing I've ever written so far. Thank you for being my sounding board when I felt stuck and my cheerleaders when I needed a boost. Love you both!

Those who attended my Get Organized session about the Six Week Sprint: I wasn't even sure this message would resonate, so I tested it on you! Your sweet comments and emails gave me a big dose of courage to finish the book. I loved seeing the passion this message inspired in you. Thank you for sharing your valuable feedback.

NOTES

Introduction
1. Dyson, James. "About Dyson", accessed April 2, 2021, https://www.npr.org/2019/07/19/743512256/dyson-james-dyson
2. Shapiro, Stephen. "Interesting New Year's Resolutions Statistics", published December 2008. accessed April 13, 2021, https://stephenshapiro.com/interesting-new-years-resolution-statistics/

Chapter 1: The Goal-Driven Life
1. O'Reilly Davi-Digui, Krista. "What if All I Want is a Mediocre Life?" accessed April 2, 2021, https://nosidebar.com/mediocre-life/
2. Virginia Sports Hall of Fame, in commenting on Arthur Ashe's induction, accessed April 2, 2021, https://steemit.com/success/@efongym/inspirationalquotesuccessisajourneynotadestination-arthurashe-h215twc9as

Chapter 2: Setting Goals that Matter
1. "4am" Delta Commercial, video, accessed April 2, 2021, https://dailycommercials.com/delta-4-m-advert/
2. Starbucks Coffee Company, "Culture and Values," accessed April 2, 2021, https://www.starbucks.com/careers/working-at-starbucks/culture-and-values

Chapter 6: How to Find Internal Motivation
1. Porterfield, Amy. "How to Create Content Rituals to Get More Done," accessed April 2, 2021. https://www.amyporterfield.com/2016/03/how-to-create-content-rituals-to-get-more-done/

2. Fogg, BJ. quoted by Astrid Groenewegen in "Motivation," accessed April 2, 2021. https://suebehaviouraldesign.com

Chapter 7: How to Harness External Motivation

1. Mischel, Walter. "The Marshmallow Experiment," accessed on April 12, 2021. https://www.simplypsychology.org/marshmallow-test.html
2. American Society of Training and Development. "The Power of Accountability," accessed on April 20, 2021. https://www.afcpe.org/news-and-publications/the-standard/2018-3/the-power-of-accountability/
3. Seinfeld, Jerry. "Don't Break the Chain," accessed on April 12, 2021. https://www.asianefficiency.com/productivity/dont-break-chain/

Chapter 8: Live a Life Without Regrets

1. Ware, Bronnie. "Regrets of the Dying," accessed on April 2, 2021. https://bronnieware.com/blog/regrets-of-the-dying/

About the Author

Kalyn Brooke is the best-selling author of Brainbook: Bullet Journaling Your Way to a More Organized Life and the founder of KalynBrooke.com, where she helps multi-passionate women embrace a more minimalist lifestyle, establish planning systems and routines, and pursue positive personal growth.

But to those who know her best, she's a self-proclaimed recovering perfectionist who lives for the fresh start of Mondays and is happiest when curled up with a page-turning book or hiking a nearby trail. The best days involve both.

Kalyn currently travels full-time with her husband, Joseph, and two bunnies in their remodeled RV. You can send her a personal message at Kalyn@KalynBrooke.com or say hello on Instagram @KalynBrookeCo.

Your road to success starts with

THE SIX-WEEK SPRINT
GOAL PLANNER

In this practical companion guide, you'll get
front-row access to this proven and proprietary
six-week framework.

Your planner includes:

- A comprehensive Life Inventory Assessment
- Intuitive questions to help narrow down your most
  important goal
- Enough Six-Week Sprint worksheets to last almost
  an entire year
- A valuable review process for every Six-Week Sprint,
  plus guidance for goal reassessments

GET YOURS AT
PRACTICALDREAMERBOOK.COM/PLANNER